GORE FAMILY TREE ○○○

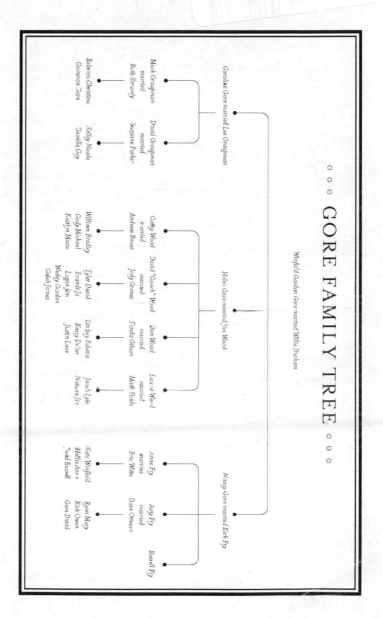

Giving up

GORE

Giving up
GORE

when our worst fear became our greatest gift

AMY & DAVE OTTESON

TATE PUBLISHING
AND ENTERPRISES, LLC

Published by Tate Publishing & Enterprises, LLC
127 E. Trade Center Terrace | Mustang, Oklahoma 73064 USA
1.888.361.9473 | www.tatepublishing.com

Tate Publishing is committed to excellence in the publishing industry. The company reflects the philosophy established by the founders, based on Psalm 68:11,
"The Lord gave the word and great was the company of those who published it."

Book design copyright © 2013 by Tate Publishing, LLC. All rights reserved.
Cover design by Allen Jomoc
Interior design by Jomel Pepito
Cover photography by Jennifer Johnson

Published in the United States of America

ISBN: 978-1-62510-933-0
1. Biography & Autobiography / Personal Memoir
2. Religion / Christian Life / Personal Growth
13.03.05

CONTENTS

Part One:
The Road to the Ditch

When you pass through the waters, I will be with you; and when you pass through the rivers, they will not sweep over you.

Isaiah 43:2 (NIV)

INTRODUCTION:
THE DITCH

*I*t was cold—so cold. Even with the sunlight coming through the water. I made out the images of the two people above me, but I couldn't rise up and break free. It was holding me down, rushing over me. The water was too strong.

It happened in an instant. It was my turn to drop the rubber ducky into the irrigation ditch at the bridge and return to the two planks one hundred feet downstream. Those planks of old wood had been there as long as I could remember—all of my seven years of age. We spent hours on those trusty boards, throwing rocks when the water was low, laughing, searching for driftwood, and daydreaming. They were weathered and gray by the long winters and swayed from the water lapping over them when the ditch was running high.

On that day years ago, the planks were our catching spot. We would take turns dropping the duck and then run as fast as we could to retrieve it. As I approached the old planks at full speed and turned onto the boards, my foot slipped off the right side. Even though it was summertime, *the cold of the water took my breath away as I fell. Although I knew how to swim, my little body was no match for the strong current. As I watched from underneath, I hoped my sister, Anne, and my cousin, Laurie, realized that I fell in. Even with their focus on the incoming duck, they would've heard the splash, right?*

Suddenly, Laurie lifted me out of the water. I gasped for breath. What had only been a few seconds seemed like slow-moving minutes. It was a hard-earned lesson, but I now knew the strength of the ditch that ran through our property. Although it wasn't an actual river itself, the ditch was powered by the might of the Gunnison River. Pulling me down and sweeping me away wouldn't have been difficult with its fast flow and depth...

THE PATRIARCH: WINFIELD GORDON GORE

Winfield Gordon Gore, born June 28, 1913, was one of those people you wouldn't forget. He had a presence that was memorable. He was an All Pro for the Los Angeles Bulldogs and then played a year for the Detroit Lions when professional football was in its infancy. No one ever called him Winfield or Gordon. He was just Gore or "Cake" as his friends called him—a nickname given to him by his sister when he was little, a moniker formed because he was "sweet as cake." I didn't think of him as "sweet." To me, he was tough but amiable. He could fix anything from a lawn mower to a shotgun to a car or a roof that needed to be repaired. Gore had married his college sweetheart and when he lost her to cancer in 1968, he never remarried. He spent time in his garden, hunted, golfed, and fly-fished as much as possible. He was a doer—not one to sit around and let time go by. He always had something in his hands—a pocketknife, a reel, a shotgun, a hoe, a drill...you name it. If it was manly and outdoorsy, he had it. My granddad was funny and ornery, but in a good way. I remember how he used to tease me:

"Amy, you must be beating all the boys in tennis. Am I right?"

"Amy, are you gonna be a great basketball player like your mom?" He then would rest his hand on my short head. I'm only five feet tall, so we both knew this sport probably wasn't in my future.

Gore let things roll off his back. Even if something bothered him, he would never let you know it. He would just press on, right up to the day that he had an aortic aneurysm at the age of seventy-three. On the day of his funeral, I felt sad and cheated that I had only gotten to know him for fourteen years. After the service, I walked into his kitchen where several people were gathered, telling Gore stories. By the end of the next hour, everyone was laughing and smiling as they all told about their adventures with Gore. As much as I grieved my loss, I knew my granddad would live on as a cherished memory.

He had lived his life to the fullest. For many of those years, he was a principal and football coach in a small Oklahoma town, but every summer he would take his family to a special place in Colorado called Jennings Ranch.

THE PLACE:
JENNINGS RANCH

Back then Jennings was just a bunch of old fishing cabins, on about forty acres of land, north of Gunnison, Colorado. My granddad took my grandmother, my mom, and her two sisters there as they grew up. Mrs. Jennings ran the place, and when she got too old to take care of the property, she inquired if my granddad Gore wanted to buy it.

"I'm gettin' too old to manage this kind of upkeep," he said. "But maybe my girls would be interested." Thankfully for us, my mom and her sisters couldn't let it go, and Jennings became a permanent part of the Gore family. After all these years, the traditions continue. Every summer, all of us gather for as long as we can to enjoy the mountains, the rivers, the hiking, the family togetherness, and of course, the fly-fishing. Fishing cabins from the early 1900s are still scattered throughout the property, and a snake-like irrigation ditch cuts through it, flowing from the mighty force of the Gunnison River. If you step outside the cabins, you see the green ranchland of the valley floor framed by the backdrop of the mountain range. Narrow footpaths mark the well-worn shortest routes between the cabins, barns, the river, and the ditch.

This place, so close to our hearts, seems to us one of God's finest creations. We forget that the beautiful, sweet-smelling wild roses have fierce, tiny thorns. We embrace the bright sunshine and brief showers and ignore the aggressive mosquitoes. We are grateful for the huge cottonwood trees with their cooling afternoon shade and dismiss the sneezing and itchy eyes that plague us when they shed their cotton. It is our place. Without realizing it, we often work more than we play. Logs need to be oiled, fences mended, cabins repaired, but we love every minute of it. We brag on each other, tease each other, help each other, and, occasionally, aggravate each other. We're an ordinary family richly blessed with this extraordinary place.

The Gore side of the family had spent time every summer at Jennings Ranch. In our younger years, all the cousins would float the river, fish, camp out, play capture the flag, build forts, and run from dawn 'til dusk. Some nights my identical twin cousins, David (or "Coach" as we all call him) and Don Wood, would tell the scariest ghost stories they could imagine about Jennings to make the rest of us sleep uneasily at night. I was the next to youngest, but our activities were such that age seldom mattered. The game of the moment simply morphed to accommodate the participants. Cathy and Laurie were as much fun as their brothers, so there was plenty of mischief. Sometimes the Graupman boys were there or the Fry cousins from my dad's side of the family would visit. It was kid heaven. Now each of us have families of our own; their kids, much older than mine, repeat the cycle. They run from morning to night and usually take our kids with them—just the way it used to be.

When my dad retired several years ago, he and my mom moved to their beloved Colorado. They spend several months in Gunnison, and we love the excuse to retreat there. It's ironic that this story begins at Jennings Ranch—a place we might have never been blessed enough to have if it hadn't been so special to my granddad, our son's namesake.

The Namesake:
Gore David Otteson

The tough and lovable spirit of Granddad Gore wasn't absent from our family for long. In 2000, I met my husband, Dave, on a blind date. A few years after graduating from the University of Washington, he moved to Denver in 1995. Within fourteen months of our first date, we were married and settled in Denver. In 2004, we started our family, and on September 22, 2008, we welcomed our third child, Gore David Otteson, into the world. When we were choosing a name for the life growing inside of me, I polled my family to make sure that it was okay to use Gore's name should we have a boy. It felt almost wrong—like we were taking an athlete's jersey number that had been retired. We didn't want to step on sacred ground. God must have known how appropriate the name was, but we had no idea how much this child was going to live up to his name.

Gore was a force to be reckoned with and performed as a typical two year old. He was precocious, sneaky, strong, and lived his life without fear. He even turned his mouth up on one side with an impish, crooked smile, the way my granddad used to. He put one hand on his hip and cocked his head as if he were Winfield "Cake" Gore incarnate.

God, please instill our Gore with a little fear, I would pray. Gore invented mischief like he was paid to do it. Before he was two, he loved to hide everything in the floor air vents.

"Gore, where's the computer mouse?" asked Dave, looking under every pile of paper on the oak desk and through all the bookshelves. We had a wireless mouse, which only made it easier for Gore to snatch and hide at his will.

Gore turned his rosy-cheeked, blond head toward Dave with that look in his eye.

"That's his giveaway," I reminded Dave. "Come on, Gore. Let Daddy have the mouse back."

Gore began what we call his "sneaky run"—on his tiptoes, with his hands covering his mouth, and pattered away with little steps toward our floor vent. He squatted down, diaper peeking over his jeans, and quickly removed the cover. With his whole arm down the vent as far as he could reach, he produced the missing mouse.

"If you didn't have that goofy smile plastered on your face all the time, I might actually get irritated with all your antics," I said, suspecting I should be more of a disciplinarian but too amused to mind.

Fortunately for Gore, we aren't adding up all the things he's destroyed. We've replaced carpet, duvet covers, upholstered chairs, vacuums, and the list goes on.

Always so affectionate, Gore would immediately turn on his charm when he sensed he did something wrong. He'd wrap his arms around my neck as tightly as he could and pat me on the back, as if to make *me* feel better about what he had done.

Unlike our other children, Gore wasn't a great sleeper. He would regularly come in about 2:30 a.m. and crawl into bed with us. Never had our other two children slept in our room, let alone our bed. As always, Gore persuasively and tightly wrapped his arms around my neck, breathed right on my face, and drifted back to sleep. I began to wonder when I was ever going to sleep through the night again.

By contrast, every afternoon Gore naps like clockwork. One afternoon, I had just settled into the office to try to follow up on some things I needed to get done. Beginning to hear what sounded like little footsteps, I got up to see if Gore left his bed. I went to his room and saw that his door was still closed. Satisfied that it was nothing, I walked back to the office. About ten minutes later, I started hearing rustling noises in the kitchen.

I called out. "Gore?"

Suddenly it was very quiet. "Gore?" I called again, pushing the chair back from the desk and standing up.

I passed into the kitchen and didn't see him. About to turn and walk out, I heard a small giggle. Then I caught a glimpse of Gore's feet standing on the counter pressed together as closely as possible against the refrigerator.

"I see you, Gore. Get down off the counter," I said firmly.

No movement and no response. I marched over to him. He had opened up the cabinet and was hiding behind it. His face and upper body were covered, his legs were in plain view, but he *thought* I couldn't see him. Scattered around his feet were several chocolate wrappers. From what I could tell, he had eaten at least seven Hershey Kisses. I swung open the cabinet door. He stood motionless with his eyes closed and the biggest smile on his face—a chocolate ring smeared around his grin.

Fighting back my laughter, I attempted to sound stern, "Gore, I can see you. You can open your eyes now."

Opening his eyes, he giggled. Then, thinking he was actually surprising me, he shouted, "Boo!"

His greatest joy and recreation was playing tricks while trying to stay on my good side. One look at him, and all I could do was laugh and sweep him into my arms. With Gore, our family was complete.

THE TEST:
BRING THE RAIN

Prior to the events of the 2010 Fourth of July weekend, I was extremely cautious and fearful when it came to our children. Trying to better cope with this fear, I had begun to pray specifically to loosen my grip on them. A few years prior, Dave's sister, Sherri, said to me, "Our children are not ours. They are a gift, just like everything else." Initially, I was annoyed with this way of thinking. I respected her and her insight, but I couldn't agree. I could give everything else up—but *not* my kids. They were mine, and my job was to protect them. I could keep them safe every day, so I thought.

In May, just two months before Gore's accident, I was jogging along the picturesque mountains just outside of Gunnison. Towering, lush green trees dotted both sides of the trail. You could lose yourself staring at the big blue sky with potbellied puffs of cloud. Running is therapeutic—my escape to clear my head, pray, and process. Submerged in thought, iPod on, my interest piqued at the lyrics of Mercy Me's song "Bring the Rain":

> *The question just amazes me*
> *Can circumstances possibly*
> *Change who I forever am in You...*
>
> *And I know there'll be days*
> *When this life brings me pain*
> *But if that's what it takes to praise You*
> *Jesus, bring the rain*

Why can't I get this out of my mind? I thought. *God, could circumstances change who I am in You? Could I praise You if You "brought the rain"?* I began to dwell on the potential of this phrase. All my life, even in the worst of times, I've held close and true to God. Easy for me I suppose, I was blessed with three happy and healthy children and a wonderful husband. I had never experienced something terribly traumatic or tragic. The lyrics resonated in my mind: *"But if that's what it takes to praise You, Jesus, bring the rain."*

Both fearful and hopeful, I began to pray. I was hit with the realization of the faith I was placing in God. Maybe it was not a prayer that I should have prayed, but the lyrics challenged me. I had no idea what it was to suffer or experience real pain in my life.

God, test me. I want to know that my faith in You will never waiver. And better yet, I want this faith to grow stronger. A daring request, but I needed to believe with all my heart that no matter what, I could stand on God's promises of who He says He is. I knew to my core God was sovereign, and He took care of me in spite of myself—certainly not because I deserve it, but because I have been saved by grace. *Completely* unmerited and undeserved. I understood the outcome of my relationship with Christ. "Test me. I will stay close to You. I *know* it."

And yet a haunting thought crept into my mind. I tried to brush it away but couldn't…

Please just don't involve my children.

That was my one condition, as if I should be placing conditions on God. God, in all His sovereignty, already cemented plans that would soon go into motion. I was about to draw on every bit of faith instilled in me and be tested, indeed.

Loosening my grip on the children was an arduous task. Ryan, our oldest at five, was our rule follower. She usually stayed out of trouble and kept her brothers in line. Kirk, named after my dad, was only fourteen months younger than Ryan and was the polar opposite of Gore. Kirk was so mellow and docile as a baby that I worried about him until he became a typical two-year-old. Gore was a different breed. Almost from the beginning, we knew we had to be on our toes at all times. He became more mischievous and danger seeking with age. Having us chase him was like a game; we were convinced that we might have a track star on our hands. If he got a head start, it took a dead run for me to catch up to him, and he would be laughing the whole way. He would live every minute outside if we allowed it—a tall order during the Colorado wintertime. But still, he looked for every opportunity to escape.

It was this pursuit of mischief that led to the beginning of a bad nightmare.

PART TWO:
THE ACCIDENT

THE TRAGEDY:
JULY 6, 2010

AMY

Most years there are about forty of our family members and friends that cook out at Jennings to celebrate the Fourth of July. To know my family is an adventure in itself. There are almost as many interesting and inspiring stories as there are characters. Together they form an incredibly strong and colorful network of love and support. Each year we eagerly anticipate this time together. After we eat too many hamburgers and way too much Texas Pie, the sun sets, and we head into Gunnison for the fireworks display. Our fun and games of the weekend had just ended; it was Tuesday, July 6, 2010, the date forever branded in my mind.

In the summer, I regularly take our kids to Jennings for several weeks at a time, and Dave travels back and forth from our home in Denver. He works in his office for three or four days and then works and plays from the cabin the next three or four. That Tuesday morning, he had gone back to Denver after the long weekend.

The kids always miss their daddy when he leaves, but they have plenty of cousins to keep them entertained. In the meantime, I hold down the fort.

Just on the other side of the mountain, my dear friend, Mary Lynn, was up from Texas visiting her family's cabin. We decided that she should drive over for the afternoon and night so our kids could play and we could visit. Mary Lynn and I had lived together after college in both Dallas and Denver, we were engaged two days apart, and we got married two weeks apart. Our lives parallel in so many ways—if something good or bad happened to one of us, we began to joke that the other one better get ready for what's on the horizon. For both of us being so small in stature, we are very strong willed—"Dynamite in small packages," as my dad would say. We both have straightforward, candid personalities and "tell it like it is"—except when she speaks her mind, it's in a strong Texas drawl. We know each other for the good and the bad, and after twenty years of friendship, she knows me as well as anyone could.

Although we saw each other fairly often in Denver or Texas, she hadn't visited our property in Gunnison in seven years. Not ten minutes after they arrived, the kids ran to the boat shed to play in the raft while we followed along and chatted.

"Now remind me of where the ditch is. I don't see it," Mary Lynn said.

"It's just beyond those trees, behind the tall grass." I pointed. She laughed as she asked, "Do you remember the last time we were here together? We took Roy Hobbs running with us, and he fell into that ditch!"

That day quickly returned to my mind. Mary Lynn had "inherited" Roy Hobbs when she married Tommy. "I almost broke my back getting that dog from the ditch. It took both of us and all our strength to haul him out of the water."

Her green eyes focused on the ditch in the distance. "I just want to be aware of it. That whole situation scared me. I really thought Roy Hobbs was going to drown that day."

Right then, Gore nosedived off the boat trailer, halting our trip down memory lane. Mary Lynn stifled a laugh, and I shook my head.

"All right, why don't we move to the tire swing, kids?"

<hr />

It had been a fun afternoon of being outside, and the kids were a mess. We had just finished giving them baths and were trying to get them dressed in their pajamas and ready for dinner when it all began. It was 6:45 p.m.

The pitter-patter of feet echoed throughout the cabin. Two adults weren't enough for five rambunctious children. You'd think playing nonstop in the intense mountain sun would successfully exhaust them, but that wasn't the case.

"Hold still," I instructed as Gore tried to evade my makeshift net—his pajama shirt. He never wanted to be in one spot for very long. He was streaking around the cabin attempting his "Nake, nake" dance.

"No!" He was jumping and wiggling, ready to join in the fun. I managed to pin him down just long enough to get his diaper on and slide the shirt over his head. The chatter and playful screams of his siblings caught my attention.

"Stay right here, Gore," an unreasonable request for our blond wild child. Nevertheless, I must have wandered into the adjoining room to check on the others. The details are now foggy.

Gore's pants in hand, I returned to the room. He was gone.

"Gore? Where are you?" Silence.

"Gore?"

There were four other kids playing in the cabin, and I assumed he had run up to the loft to be with his brother and sister. But when he didn't answer my calls throughout the cabin, I immediately walked out onto the porch that has a screen door to the outside and saw the latch was undone; he had figured *that* one out a few days earlier. My mouth went dry, and I felt cold.

Nervously, I walked outside and craned my head toward the irrigation ditch that ran directly behind our cabin. "Irrigation ditch" is misleading. At twelve to fourteen feet wide and three to five feet deep (depending on volume), "ditch" is an understatement. In this area, it's at full capacity and runs swiftly like a powerful creek. It comes right off the rapidly running Gunnison River and winds for miles throughout farmland and then back into the Gunnison. There is a gate that the farmers use to regulate water flow to their hay meadows, so at this time of year it is always deep and swift. We had put "temporary" orange net fencing all along the stretch closest to the cabin as a deterrent.

I ran my eyes along the ditch, spanning over a hundred yards. I didn't see him at all. Quickly crossing over the bridge, I tried to see if he headed to my parents' cabin.

Nothing.

Maybe he ran toward the road.

The Gunnison River runs right out in front, just on the other side of the dirt road, but I thought it would be strange for him to run across the road and then to the river.

He must've seen a bird. Gore had been chasing birds all summer with no regard for where he was going. He'd see one and take off after it. I began to run around wildly, hoping to find him attempting to attack one.

As Mary Lynn and I ran around searching, everyone must have heard my cries. Quickly, my family began to appear, and they were covering every bit of the forty-acre property. My cousin, David Graupman, and his wife, Suzanne, were staying in a cabin close to ours. They were the first to hear my distress. This wasn't the usual call for Gore—this was panic. Camille, their daughter, took off down the road to my twin cousins' property a short distance away. Immediately, Coach and Don Wood's families emptied out of their cabins and joined the search.

"Gore is missing! *We can't find Gore!*" I yelled, tears already stinging my eyes. Before I knew it, people dispersed in all directions to search. While Don took off on his four-wheeler to scan parts of the ditch farther back on the property, Coach waded the ditch. Everyone was looking. David waded the opposite end of the ditch, trying to cover as much territory as possible. I began to cry knowing that something horrible had happened. Too much time had passed.

So many people are looking, I thought. *Why haven't we found him already?* I was no longer thinking clearly, just running. My thoughts drifted back to my memory of falling in the ditch long ago…now, some thirty years later, the memory replayed in my head. Just like before, I saw the sun reflecting off the water; only this time I was searching for any sign of my child. The ditch was running at its threatening full capacity. Even now, it would be hard for me to walk upright in it. In my mind, the ditch mutated into an evil opponent.

I thought longingly about the peaceful past. Just *ten* minutes ago, Gore was splashing in the bath with his brother and sister, and the world was right. Now, he was nowhere to be found. I heard myself screaming, but it didn't seem real. I crossed the bridge by our cabin and took the same path as I had thirty years before, only now there was no laughing. Running along the ditch edge to search the water, I tried to reassure myself that against all odds, he wasn't there. He *couldn't* be there. I ran to the old planks and stood at the brink, looking up and downstream. No Gore.

I don't see him in the ditch, I thought wildly. *But that's good, right? It means he's somewhere else.* I repeated this to myself to shake off my gripping fear.

I continued to pound other options into my brain to rid the ditch from my thoughts.

He's chasing a bird, or running to the boat shed to play in the raft, or running to the tractor. No, he's probably in the barn. I just didn't believe what I told myself. My legs moved, and my mind spun. No one was talking, just running in different directions. It was surreal.

People appeared, but I struggled to recognize faces. I simply threw out senseless orders. The exception was Mary Lynn's face, tense with worry, at my side.

"I've looked everywhere. Every inch of ground. Go to the river. Look. I can't find him." I lost my composure. In the background, I could hear the roar of my cousins' four-wheelers. The reality that about twenty people were looking and no one could find him paralyzed me. I looked around, trying to focus. Coach was in the ditch, trudging with his body and hands, wading farther downstream than he, Don, and David had ever gone before.

Scrambling around, I bumped right into Suzanne, as she had just searched the shower house. She grabbed hold of me.

"Where is he?" I cried, somewhere between a shriek and a moan.

"We're going to find him, Amy," said Suzanne. She looked me in the eyes with a sense of nurture and care, as if she were already absorbing my burden.

I wanted to believe it. I so *desperately* wanted to believe it. Just yesterday Suzanne was having a dance party in the loft with my kids. Why was this happening?

"No! It's been over twenty minutes! How can *twenty* people not find him in *twenty* minutes?" I sobbed desperately, uncontrollably, on her shoulder. She held me for a brief moment. *I can't imagine, don't want to… this isn't reality.* My mouth was dry, and I must have been shaking uncontrollably. Again, I recalled that day that I fell in so long ago. I was so helpless and praying my cousin and sister would see me. Gore wasn't even twenty-two months old; he would never survive a *minute* in that water. *Why can't we find him?*

In that moment, I heard the moaning. It was the sound of anguish.

Have they found him?

I instantly ran toward the sound coming from the back of the property. "Tell me what's happening!" I screamed. "I can't see you! Please, who is that? Where are you?" I found myself running barefoot through brush along the ditch when I saw the image that will forever be scarred in my mind.

Right down the middle of the irrigation ditch was the big frame of my cousin, Coach, carrying Gore in his arms.

Gore's legs were hooked over Coach's right arm, and his limp body lay across his left. He was white and lifeless, still in his pajama shirt and diaper. His head was back, his hair wet, and his face ghostly white. Nausea kicked me in the stomach. It happened—the water that I had loved so much, the ditch that had always been my playground, had taken him from me. The sound that Coach made was…agonizing. It wasn't a word or even a yell. It was a moaning cry from deep within his soul.

Without thinking about anything but the need to hold Gore, I plunged into the water, trying to move toward him with my arms stretched out. I began to feel the fiery pain—the instant regret and guilt that I had not been able to find him was drowning *me*.

He must have been wondering where I was and why I wasn't helping him. That's what mothers do—they help their children. Our job is to protect and help them in their times of need. It was the only thought I remember having: *I'm so sorry, Gore. I am so sorry that Mommy couldn't find you.*

Just as I was about to take him into my arms, I felt my dad, a retired surgeon, reach over me and take him from Coach. With Gore in his arms, Dad wailed bloodcurdling cries as he moved toward the bank. "No, God! Oh, no, God!" His usually serene face contorted in suffering.

The scene was horrific, moving in slow motion. People were dropping to their knees, crying, and praying. I couldn't believe what I was seeing; I must have transcended the situation and watched it happen to someone else because this *couldn't* have been real. This couldn't have been our Gore.

Right there amidst all the rock and fallen tree branches, dad laid Gore down on the bank. Suzanne immediately started performing CPR, alternating with my dad. For years, Suzanne has been a nurse in OB and surgery. The two people that were trained to do this were with him. Standing, frozen, I watched her body over Gore's. I saw them pushing on Gore's lungs in hopes the water would pour from his mouth, to no avail. Each second was my personal hell.

"I'm so sorry, Gore. I'm so sorry. So sorry." My cries morphed into screams. "I'm so sorry, Gore!" I couldn't stand here and watch *any* of this anymore. It was over. I had to get out of there, but I was too weak for the water, which was more like a tangled web of debris. My eyes moved toward the culverts behind me, realizing Gore's body had traveled through them, and wondered how he came out in one piece. Starting to sink to my knees at that dreadful thought, my cousin Don grabbed me and held me up. Looking around, I realized I was in the water, grasping a branch. Don wrapped me tighter in his arms and lifted me to dry ground.

"Everything's going to be okay," Don murmured as I wailed.

Each torturous minute passed dreadfully. Don began to help Suzanne and Dad perform CPR. Cries of despair and anguish filled the air. And they were all mine. It was devastating. These images chaotically swirled around me.

Amidst the aggressive actions of Suzanne tilting Gore's head and then desperately attempting to empty him of water, I saw my dad emit intense, agonal cries of despair. My sweet dad—his demeanor was normally calm and contemplative. He was always there for me, ready with words of wisdom or encouragement. *Never* had I seen him at such a loss. He knew what I knew: Gore had drowned. He fell back in utter exhaustion.

Don unfailingly persevered with Gore. "It's okay, Kirk. I'll take over from here," he said. As the hopelessness of the situation heightened, so did my agony. An agony that pulled me toward the ground and threatened to crush me.

I no longer knew what I did while they performed CPR. Instead, I was thinking of Dave. How in the world could I find enough strength to tell him Gore had drowned?

In that moment, Mary Lynn chose to stay with Gore. We had been friends long enough that she knew comforting me wouldn't be fruitful. As I pushed past her on the bank, her instinct was to remain with Gore. She knew to take my place. Automatically, her petite figure knelt down just above my dad and Suzanne. As she glanced down at them, without consciousness of what she was doing, she lifted one of her hands to the sky and left the other hand on ghostly white Gore.

Mary Lynn later explained, "My friend, Lydia, once encouraged me that when I prayed for my children, I should touch them with one hand and put the other hand in the air so that God's power can go through me to my child." At the time, she had smiled at Lydia and thought, *To each his own.* That wasn't something Mary Lynn felt the need to do until that moment on the bank when she stared down at Gore's lifeless body. Lydia's words entered her mind, and she did exactly that. She began to pray over him and the others as they gave CPR.

She said that she prayed two things. The first was from the Bible in the book of Ezekiel, "Breathe life into these dry bones," and the other was from the book of Revelation, "Holy, Holy, Holy, is the Lord God

Almighty, who was and is and is to come." Although it came out spontaneously, she repeated it over and over as they tried to resuscitate him.

Gore's face was drained of color. His lips, nose, and cheeks...all pale. Gore was known for his bright pink cheeks—it was his trademark. He ceased being Gore Otteson without them.

Suzanne stayed focused with this thought. Don nudged my dad and said, "We have to keep going." Gore's lips were still cold, but the three of them carried on with an unrelenting determination.

It seemed like ages, but in less than ten minutes, I heard the ambulance. The sirens slapped me out of my tormented stupor.

How silly that they're coming now with their sirens, as if they could do something at this point. I saw Gore when he came out of the water. I knew he had been underwater for at least twenty minutes. Not processing much at that point, I knew they had been giving him CPR from that first moment at the bank, and he still wasn't alive.

The sheriff's cars blocked off the one-way dirt road and made way for the ambulance. A paramedic shot out the back doors, ran toward the ditch, immediately scooped Gore up, and bolted back to the vehicle. They didn't waste a single second.

"Please don't leave me here," I mumbled as I watched helplessly. Suddenly, as if on cue, someone pushed me into the ambulance. Falling into the corner, muddy and wet, I rested my head on the wall as the doors slammed shut. I lay on the floor against the corner, numb.

I'm only about thirty minutes into this whole nightmare. The memory was a painful blur minus one word I heard over and over: *asystole. I've heard that on TV in hospital shows*, I thought. *It means he doesn't have a heartbeat.*

Time eluded me after that.

> The fundamental fact of existence is that this trust in God, this faith, is the firm foundation under everything that makes life worth living.
>
> Hebrews 11:1 (The Message)

DAVE

Life was business as usual. I left Gunnison at 4:00 a.m. to return to Denver for work. After a long day, I received an impromptu invitation to play softball that night and was on my way a little after 7:00 p.m., expecting lighthearted revelry, *not* the phone call I received. Peeking down at my angrily buzzing phone, I saw it was Amy's mom, Nancy. *That's weird*, I thought.

"Hello, Nancy?"

"Dave, Gore…" she broke off. At first I thought it was the spotty cell phone coverage, but I quickly realized she was sobbing. Then we *were* cut off.

What's going on? I thought nervously. Nancy called back immediately.

"Nancy, what happened?" I had a bad feeling and gripped the steering wheel with my free hand.

"Gore fell in the irrigation ditch. Kirk is working on him, but it may be too late. Can you get here?" She purged this information in one swift, broken exhale of words.

The call was over, and I now began the race of my lifetime.

When I first began to process what Nancy had said, my heart literally hurt. My adrenaline spiked crazily. First came the disbelief. "No…what? This isn't happening." I simply couldn't process the news. It was surreal, unbelievable. But before I knew it, I was crying uncontrollably, tears blinding my vision as I drove. My mind spun out of control.

But then…

Amy. Oh, God. Amy. This can't be real.

Memories flooded in: Amy rushing toward me in the driveway while I fastened Gore's car seat.

"Dave, there are tons of people in the park. Don't let the kids out of your sight for *one second*. Promise me!"

Or, "Please drive slower. You're scaring me, and we have precious cargo in here."

Amy is more devastated than I could even understand right now.

We had talked before about how the one thing that would be nearly impossible to overcome was if something happened to one of our children. And now this was our reality… *No, it couldn't be.*

I pulled over for just a second to try and collect myself…and take care of necessities. Dialing my own side of the family, I attempted to relay the news. Following their "hellos," I was unable to speak for several seconds, and then finally my voice cracked. "Gore may have drowned." I hardly remember this nightmarish exchange. What I do remember, though, is my request: "Please pray for two things. One, pray for a miracle. Two, pray for peace for Amy."

Alone, I had no idea if I was ever going to see our precious Goresky alive again (as our daughter, Ryan, affectionately called him). Even without concrete details of what transpired, I felt numb. Disbelief led to inexplicable pain, worse than any physical pain I've ever experienced.

> I am worn out waiting for your rescue, but I have put my hope in your word. My eyes are straining to see your promises come true. When will you comfort me?
>
> Psalm 119:81-82 (NLT)

Amy

We arrived at Gunnison Valley Hospital, and Gore did not have a pulse. It had been forty minutes since I last saw him in the cabin. It was astonishing how much one's life could change in such a short amount of time.

Paralyzed by grief, I was helped out of the ambulance, and someone guided me inside into a room. I didn't feel any sensations. I was a prisoner in my mind.

Why even attempt to go with Gore? It's over.

In spite of the flurry of nurses around me and the suspense of the situation, I thought about Dave, unaware that my mom had called him. Everything happened so fast that I tried to imagine *how* I'd call him and tell him this nightmare. Some nurses were trying to comfort me; their reassurances floated around my ears, but I was in shock. "We will let you know as soon as we know anything at all," one said. Her words sounded distant and muffled. My screams abated, so I was just waffling between sobbing and throwing up.

From a faraway corner in my mind, I heard voices.

"Your parents are here. They want to come in." *Yes, I want that.*

My mom and dad were in the doorway. They tried to comfort me in the midst of their own overwhelming pain.

"Amy, I already called Dave," said Mom.

Relief flooded my limbs; I was so thankful I didn't have to initiate that phone call. One of the kind nurses brought me some scrubs to change into so I could get out of my cold, wet clothes—reminders of the lamentable scene.

My mom began cleaning the caked mud off my feet. "Mom, you don't need to…" I trailed off as she shook her head toughly. *Why does she insist?* I wondered. I could see tears rolling down her cheeks the whole time, but she never broke down. I then understood. Mom, like "Cake" Gore, responded differently to these situations. Engrossing herself in the task of cleaning me up, she busied herself to accomplish what she does best: staying strong. She filled out paperwork and tried to answer the nurses' questions on my behalf. *Why couldn't I be more like that?* I needed her strength.

I don't know how long we sat in that room, but I recall my dad and I sitting on the floor crying and praying. My dad's thick gray hair was disheveled as he ran his fingers through it anxiously. I prayed God could wash my guilt away—it was merciless, choking me.

❖

The scene materialized before me. My father's face was carved with stress lines. My mom was in constant motion. She would check on me, talk to the nurses, and update our family (now gathered in the waiting room). Now she drifted in and out, waiting for any welcome distraction.

"What's going on? When can I see him?" was my first speech I managed to string together.

A nurse glanced up and said, "I'll let you know as soon as we know anything."

Why don't they know something? Mere minutes seemed like an eternity.

Suddenly, a nurse came in, knelt down next to me, and relayed what was taking place. "We have a heartbeat! We're still working on him but will let you know as soon as you can be with him. Right now we need you to keep yourself calm and let us stay focused on Gore," she said.

Moments later, I couldn't believe what I was hearing: "They're flying him by helicopter to Denver!" I sharply inhaled and was stuck between preparing myself for disappointment and wanting to run freely with hope. Tears trickled down my face once more.

"Stay right here," said Mom. "I'll go ahead and call Dave." She disappeared into the hallway as I tried to calm down. I wanted to be with Gore.

Finally, a nurse told me that I could see him. Walking into the trauma room was a moment that took my breath away. He still looked lifeless, wet, and cold, and had countless wires and equipment attached to him. Someone scooted a chair over so I could sit next to him and talk to him. At this point, we were waiting for the helicopter to arrive as they continued trying to stabilize him.

My eyes welled up. The only words that occurred to me were, "I'm so sorry, Gore. I'm sorry I didn't find you sooner." I was already down a long road of guilt and blame on myself.

The respiratory therapist spoke soothingly to me. "He's trying to take some breaths on his own, and he has a heartbeat." I turned toward her kind face and couldn't help but notice the emotion in her voice.

Suddenly, I was paralyzed. I started to feel so hopeful and then terrified to feel any optimism. After already thinking he was gone, I was afraid of having even a little hope before it all unraveled again.

Snapping me out of my reverie was a nurse trying to tell me something about the helicopter. I couldn't focus on anyone's face, too afraid to take my eyes off Gore.

"As it turns out, Mrs. Otteson, there was some miscommunication, and there is no room for you to ride on the helicopter." They dropped a bomb on me; I panicked at the thought of separating from him. One of the sheriffs behind me put his hands on my shoulders and talked me off the ledge.

"Gore needs you to be strong. After all, he's right here and can hear you. Stay calm." Right then, someone asked me if I wanted to start driving to Denver, and I thought, *No way*. I was so afraid to leave him. *What if something happens on the way to Denver and he doesn't make it? Right now he is alive, and I am staying.*

Constantly, I recycled the same thought in the back of my mind: *Three minutes…three minutes. I want just three minutes of my life back. I'm going to spend the rest of my life thinking about those few minutes that I didn't know he wasn't in the cabin.* I stared at him, thinking about what he must have been thinking. He must have wondered why I wasn't helping him. It was excruciating.

Right about that time, the team from the helicopter *CareFlight 11* arrived. The process of transferring the care of Gore from the ED (Emergency Department) staff to the flight team took about twenty minutes. Finally, when they were ready, I looked around the room at all the nameless people and tried to thank them as best I could. They were all attempting to smile and say positive things, such as, "This is good! We have a heartbeat, and he's trying to breathe on his own."

I hugged the doctor in charge, Dr. Sherman, and said, "I will bring him back when he's better." His blue eyes reflected concern, but he smiled wanly as he gave me my last moment with my son before the journey to Denver.

"Go ahead and walk him to the doors where they will take him out to the helicopter," he said. The push to save Gore's life was in full swing, and there was no time to ruminate on what might happen next. I had to make it to the next minute, and Gore had to make it to Denver.

My parents by my side, we started toward the parking lot. As we neared the entrance of the ED, I saw my entire family; everyone was there. We're close knit, so it was clear to me that their hearts were breaking. I saw my cousin Cathy, her face and eyes reddened. She hugged me as I approached the waiting room.

"Andrew and Coach are looking for you. They want to follow you to Denver." I couldn't even respond as I surveyed the statues surrounding me. My aunt Helen and uncle Jim stood quietly, sadness visible on their faces. Helen is strong like my mom; she can handle a lot, so I knew she'd be the rock for Coach, Don, and Cathy.

Although they portrayed the same positive demeanor and forced smiles that the doctors and nurses had, I regretted at that moment that my whole family had to live with this nightmare just as I did. Jennings was forever tainted. I was sure that I'd never go back.

Everyone hugged us as we went to the car.

"Tonda, Jody," I huskily called to Don and Coach's wives. "Please take care of Kirk and Ryan. Tell them whatever you think is best. I don't know what they saw, but they're probably scared."

"Of course." They both hugged me, and I knew my kids would be safe with them; no need to dwell on that.

Mom, Dad, and I made it to Dad's truck. Ominous, steel-colored clouds loomed on the horizon. We knew we'd be driving over about four mountain passes. This was not a drive to tackle at night, *especially* not for people in our state of mind.

"I want to drive," I managed. "No!" was the immediate response from my parents. We were four solid hours from the hospital in Denver. About halfway there, the cracks of lightning and hail added to the stress of the drive.

Have mercy on me, O God, have mercy on me, for in you my soul takes refuge. I will take refuge in the shadow of your wings until the disaster has passed.

Psalm 57:1 (NIV)

DAVE

For forty minutes, I hauled our SUV to Gunnison. I wept the whole way.

Suddenly, Nancy called again.

Is she calling me back because he died? The abhorrent thought flashed across my mind as my trembling hand grabbed the phone.

"Dave, they got a heartbeat. They're flying him to the Children's Hospital in Denver. That's all we know right now." Like a reflex, I jerked the steering wheel, turned around, and sped toward that hospital. My mind was in a fog as I continued to plead with God. I hysterically screamed into my windshield, "Don't take him!" It was excruciating pain, not knowing if I could ever hold Gore again and being so unsure how our family and *especially* Amy would survive this.

The thought of Gore not being with us was simply too insurmountable to fathom. I could picture him with his big, infectious smile. My mind reflected on his affinity for the extreme. When he went outside to ride his bike or anything that moved, we would put a helmet on him—not just a bike helmet but often a *full ski helmet*. He'd still somehow manage to fly over the handlebars and land on his face, leaving him scraped and bleeding from chin to forehead. Remarkably, danger always found him.

Only this time, he might not be so lucky.

Gore's face in my memory kept me focused, even though the sky was black and pouring rain. Heavy construction forced me to detour, but my clouded mind somehow navigated me into the emergency entrance of Children's. I registered with the security personnel while trying to hold back tears.

"Dave Otteson." They called my name. I was then introduced to a social worker who led me back to a room to wait while I struggled to wrap my mind around what was happening.

The social worker pushed her coat sleeve back and glanced at her watch. "It's going to be about an hour and fifteen minutes before the helicopter arrives. Once Gore is in the trauma room, we'll come get you."

Time stopped. Someone came in and told me that some friends from church were here, and I was surprised. I had made a few phone calls prior to arriving at the hospital appealing for prayer, but I hadn't asked anyone to be there.

After dragging myself to the waiting room, I was glad to see a few buddies from our old church and a couple from our Sunday school class. It helped having someone there with me as I continued trying to process the events from the last two hours.

"Dave," said my friend Todd. He waved and I walked over. Not much was said initially; he gave me a bear hug, and we sat in silence. But conversation sneaked up on us.

"I tell ya what, when I was here about a year ago, I learned what food tastes good and what's 'blah.' You have to get one of the breakfast burritos, 'The Beast,' I think it's called. It's the size of a football." Small talk, but I know what he was trying to do. As Amy and I reflected on these events, we know people often don't know what to say. There are no words. Their intentions are kind, but we often can't speak in the face of the anguish. What mattered is that our friends were there.

How can I be strong at a moment like this? I remember reciting this in my mind and vividly watching a woman from our church named Kathy aimlessly walk around the hospital in a trance, knowing she was reaching out to God. Kathy is someone who reminds me of my late grandmother, who has the type of faith that gives her a special direct pipeline to our Maker. As one of the most prayerful people I know, I knew she understood what I needed more than anything right then: prayer. And *lots* of it. She is well aware of what the power of prayer can do. One Sunday, she shared with Amy and me about miraculous things she witnessed while helping in the prayer rooms of our church—all authentic and amazing. Of course, she would never accept credit for having any part of it. It was always all God. But if you ask me, Kathy's gift is that she has the faith to pray for such things, a faith that will move mountains. Therefore, her presence soothed me.

> "You don't have enough faith," Jesus told them. "I tell you the truth, if you had faith even as small as a mustard seed, you could say to this

mountain, 'Move from here to there,' and it would move. Nothing would be impossible."

Matthew 17:20 (NLT)

AMY

As we got in the truck for the longest car ride of our lives, my first thought was that I had to call Dave. *He doesn't know how bad it is. I have to tell him and prepare him for what he's about to see.* In my dad's truck was a bag that Mary Lynn had packed for me with a few things, one being my cell phone. After being shut out of the helicopter, it felt like a lifeline. Knowing I had only a few minutes before we'd be out of cell range, I tried to collect myself and call Dave. The phone barely rang once when I heard Dave answer.

"Amy!"

As soon as I heard my husband's voice, I sobbed. His voice was an anchor that dragged me to new depths of my despair with the realization that my mistake so deeply affected the man I loved. Between my cries, all I could say was that I was sorry. Nothing else came to mind.

"Amy, it's not your fault," he assured me softly through unmistakable tears. "I'm never going to blame you. It was an accident."

I knew I needed to let him know how bad it was. I kept thinking that he hadn't seen what I did and couldn't begin to understand.

"I couldn't find him. He was under water *so* long."

He was quiet. We were both devastated. Static kept interrupting the little conversation we had, so I said, "Just please let me know once Gore arrives. Please."

The drive was plagued with my cries and screams almost the entire time. It was the closest thing that I know to losing it. What I didn't know was that my cousins, Coach and Andrew, were following us. Mom's phone rang. In between my weeping, I could hear their voices saying, "Can...drive to Denver."

"No, we have it taken care of. Go ahead and turn around," Mom pled.

They refused. "We're not going anywhere."

I would get an occasional text from them of encouragement, but I knew what this was doing to them. Even with a caravan of support, I felt far from comforted.

The suspense clung to me. "I need to know as soon as Gore's there," I repeated loudly to my parents. Between my tears, I'd peer at the bars on my phone and call Dave the second I got service.

"Is Gore there yet?"

"No. Not yet."

Each time I heard that, the knots in my stomach grew tighter and tighter. Each minute dragged torturously.

I sobbed in the back seat. "I can't take this." Between screams, my parents had no idea what to tell me. Dad funneled all his energy into driving carefully in the weather over each mountain pass.

But then, finally, came the call, "Gore just arrived in Denver."

"Wait, what?" I said on the edge of my seat.

"They're all…on…" I couldn't understand Dave. The bad connection kept interfering.

"Dave, you're breaking up. Say it again."

"They're working on him—can't tell what's happening. I'll call you soon." Then the call would drop, and I was left with the silence. I'd call right back. He wouldn't answer. *Is this because something bad happened and he doesn't want to tell me over the phone?* I thought, alarmed. This was absolute torture.

> We are pressed on every side by troubles, but we are not crushed. We are perplexed, but not driven to despair. We are hunted down, but never abandoned by God. We get knocked down, but we are not destroyed.
>
> 2 Corinthians 2:8-9 (NLT)

Dave

Soon, a nurse came in. "Dave, Gore just arrived, if you'd like to come with us." Anxiously, I took a deep breath and thought, *Here we go, God. You have already scripted what is to come. I am not in control of what is next.* I felt for Amy as I shared in her crippling pain despite not being together, knowing it was agonizing not being there with Gore and me.

Escorted by a team of nurses, I walked into the horrific scene of Gore lying on a trauma table with about fifteen doctors, nurses, paramedics, assistants, and respiratory therapists all working on him. There were another fifteen or so people just outside the room, watching the tragedy unfold. Gore's arms were moving stiffly with convulsive, robotic-like movements, clinically called posturing. I thought this was a positive sign that he was moving, only to find out it's usually a sign of severe brain damage. There were three doctors in the room who introduced themselves brusquely and gave a quick summary of Gore's condition.

"I am extremely nervous about the outcome of this."

"There's a less than *one-percent chance* that he will ever walk or talk again."

"He has been through a traumatic event and is in seriously critical condition."

Those comments blew me away as I watched them continue to work. Gore was still cold from the episode, and they were trying to warm him closer to a normal temperature. Feeling as cold as Gore, my mind was on pause. All that circulated were four magnified words: *less than one percent.*

Less than one percent.

My mouth was dry, and I was numb. I now knew the true importance of praying for a miracle because that was precisely what it would take. *A miracle.*

Gore was on a ventilator to help him breathe and was cold and unresponsive except for his erratic posturing movements. I didn't know if Amy knew the severity of the situation we were in, and she was probably still two hours away with spotty cell coverage. *How can I tell her the new information?*

One doctor walked up to me and said, "Mr. Otteson, we're going to take him up to CT and then to the PICU," or Pediatric Intensive Care Unit. I could only helplessly follow, watch, listen, and wait.

I believe in the sun, even when it's not shining.
I believe in love even when I do not feel it. I
believe God, even when He is silent.

Author Unknown

AMY

Finally, the text I'll never forget arrived: "Gore is critical and headed to CT and then PICU." The text branded itself in my mind. I was in a state that, even now, is almost impossible to discuss. Emotions I can't relive pulled me down into a void of unspeakable dejection. I *needed* to be in Denver.

During one of my downward spirals, feeling I could never forgive myself and Dave shouldn't either, my mom quietly spoke. "Dave doesn't have it in him to blame you. It's just not in his makeup. That is why it is better that *you* were with Gore rather than Dave."

That hit me like a bag of bricks. "That's hard to hear," I said softly. But in my heart of hearts, I knew she was right. It would forever be about *me* trying to forgive myself, not Dave trying to forgive me. I remembered hounding Dave about our kids.

"Watch them closely."

"Don't let them out of your sight."

"Drive slower! Kids are in the car!"

"Don't forget Gore needs this, Kirk needs that…"

Enough, I told myself. *I know that if Dave were in my place, I'd ask him what in the world he was doing to lose one of our children.* I felt ashamed; I felt like an awful person.

I thought back to my fearfulness and the phrase, "Our children are not ours. They are a gift, just like everything else." At the time I heard that phrase, I began reading a book by Stormy O'Martian called *Power of a Praying Parent.* In it, she discusses being able to understand that God loves our children more than we do. Convicted about this, I acknowledged I was being a control freak. There is no way that I was ever going to be able to be everywhere and constantly protect our children. I *had* to let go and trust that God loved them more than I did. It's much easier said than done, but I knew that I needed to work toward that.

When Gore's accident happened, I obviously hadn't mastered my control issues with the kids. Each and every day, I tried not obsessing every time I left the kids or instructing Dave on what to do, or exactly what not to do, when they were solely in his care. Now, here I sat on my way to the hospital, realizing that the ever-fearful overprotector had been in charge when the worst ordeal that had ever happened occurred.

Why do I have to be so stubborn? All that worrying and fear had done nothing, I thought. *I had no more control in this situation. Don't I believe in God's sovereignty and His will? I absolutely think that I do, so why can't I open up my hand and let go of this control and fear? Why can't I trust that God loves them more than I do?*

It was time. God was going to refine me one way or the other. I don't get to pick and choose what I relinquish to Him.

As we got about an hour outside of Denver, threatening charcoal-colored clouds scarred the sky. It was raining, hailing, and lightning. *How often do we get that in Denver? Not a whole lot. No wonder it took the helicopter so long.*

I started to wrestle with God. "Seriously, what are You doing? The storm is adding time to our drive." I wasn't blaming Him, but I felt conflicted. I wanted answers. I wanted to understand why this was happening, and as humans, we just can't.

> "My thoughts are nothing like your thoughts," says the Lord. "And my ways are far beyond anything you can imagine. For just as the heavens are higher than the earth, so my ways are higher than your ways and my thoughts higher than your thoughts."
>
> Isaiah 55:8-9 (NLT)

DAVE

After his CT scan, Gore was admitted to the PICU on the third floor. His prognosis was based on several things: the amount of time that he wasn't breathing and had been without a heartbeat, the temperature of the water was not cold enough to be protective, his posturing movements, fixed pupils, an abnormal EEG (the EEG monitored his brain activity), and the acidosis in his blood. The most likely outcome was a child having severe neurological deficiencies and never being able to perform basic tasks like eating, walking, or talking. The outcome was grim.

Wow. Being strong for Amy was becoming increasingly difficult to accomplish. *She has intuition that is uncanny; she'll know immediately.*

I walked downstairs to meet her, stomach churning and palms cold. She was getting close. I approached the security desk in hopes of saving Amy the customary "Show us your ID" routine.

"Please just print her out a name badge," I coaxed. "She's going to be anxious to see our son and get an update on his condition." My pleading must've worked because he didn't argue.

Waiting for Amy to walk in, I thought about my game plan. While the doctors had communicated to me just how bad of shape Gore was in, I felt that my role was to be more supportive to Amy than to communicate the "less than one-percent chance of walking and talking" line emblazoned in my mind.

God only knows what that prognosis will do to her.

Walking outside, I halted as I saw Amy's dad's truck swerve into the driveway. Amy threw open the door and turned her head to me. Her face was red and tear streaked; her hair was unkempt. All I could think was, *Be strong for Amy. Be strong, Dave.* I knew Amy well enough to know that she was not going to want to talk to anyone. She briefly greeted our friends that came but kept her eyes at an unknown fixed point in the distance.

My energy suddenly drained. I felt like someone else's feet carried me to Amy, someone else's arms encircled her small frame close to me, and someone else whispered, "It's not your fault. It never was and never will be your fault." My hands patted rhythmically with my words of reassurance.

"Trust me. *It's not your fault.*"

> For no one is cast off by the Lord forever. Though he brings grief, he will show compassion, so great is his unfailing love. For he does not willingly bring affliction or grief to anyone.
>
> Lamentations 3:31-33 (NIV)

AMY

We went directly to Gore's room. I thought I would be prepared to see him again, but he was just as before. He looked lifeless, pallid with a dismal gray hue, only now he had more wires and tubes attached to him. My stomach rose to my throat.

Dave already talked to numerous doctors that night, but the one in charge in the PICU was Dr. Jesse. He had cropped hair and was all business. He began with, "We're going to do everything we can to make him comfortable." For me that translated into, "We are going to wait for him to die."

"How bad is it?" I asked softly but directly. I was too tired for anything but the facts.

"It's extremely bad."

I pushed. "Just tell me how bad it is." I knew what I had seen and how bad I thought it was, but I was not prepared for what he said next. In a split second, I had a thought that they were going to say that he had a 30 or 40 percent chance.

The response that will ring in my ears forever: "He has a less than one-percent chance of ever having any brain function." I felt Dave's grip tighten around me as I involuntarily started sinking to the ground.

It is strange that in that one second I had time to think about what I thought I was going to hear, but that wasn't it. In shock, I clung to Dave as he held me up. I was truly unable to grasp that this was happening. Dr. Jesse left us alone with Gore.

Within a few minutes, he returned.

"We're going to try something." He had our attention. "We don't think it will make any difference, but we want to give him every chance we can." I thought that those words seemed odd but was too scared, tired, and numb to question anything. When you've been told less than one percent, you are looking for *anything* to try. We said, "Do it." It wasn't ever a decision that we discussed or questioned; it couldn't get worse than what it was. Less than one percent was equivalent to zero.

After pushing for authorization to do the hypothermic treatment, Dr. Jesse began to explain what was involved.

"It's where the body is lowered to ninety degrees to minimize brain activity. It has to be done for forty-eight hours. We will monitor everything constantly, and if at any point any of his organs appear to be shutting down or he starts having seizures, then we have to abort the protocol."

Our understanding was that it had been used to some extent previously, but there wasn't a lot of information on someone of Gore's age and condition.

They had more data and *some* success in adult cardiac arrest patients and newborns. We later learned that this protocol had been implemented only two months prior with only three cases in the PICU…and none with good results. None of this mattered. We were willing to try absolutely anything, but what we really needed was a miracle.

What inspired the "cooling" was information from our nurse Lily, who was in the trauma room with Gore when he arrived. She believed she might have seen Gore make a purposeful movement while she was re-taping his vent tube. His arm had suddenly jerked toward his mouth.

Based on his lack of any verbal, motor, or pupil response and the sheer medical facts, this was inconsistent with everything else he had done. Lily communicated to the doctor staff that his movement toward his tube appeared intentional, and that's when Dr. Jesse fought for further treatment.

After the information overload, I crumpled to the hallway floor and began to cry. I looked to my left, where Dave was sitting next to me, and to my right were Coach and Andrew. They both stared through the all-glass front wall of Gore's room. Coach had tears rolling down his face yet was trying to console me. For the first time, a terrible thought crept in. The reality of the situation was foreboding…

Andrew and Coach had each lost a son many years before. Coach and his wife, Jody, had a son, Logan, who was stillborn. Andrew and his wife, Cathy, had also lost a son, Cody, after his third birthday. He was born with many issues, and they knew that they might only get to have him for a little while. These were both very different circumstances than this, but it didn't matter: they had to bury their child. I suddenly found myself regretful that I hadn't been more sensitive or understanding at the time when they were at such loss. Yes, I was younger and I didn't have children of my own yet, but I felt sorry that, until now, I had no concept of what they had been through.

Did they feel like I do right now? I know You're here, Lord. Did You leave people with me who also lost a son because I'm about to lose mine? As I sat trying to process this, I began to pray at that moment for a miracle. *God, please intercede and change this outcome. I know You can if it's Your will.*

> In the same way, the Spirit helps us in our weakness. We do not know what we ought to pray for, but the Spirit himself *intercedes* for us through wordless groans.
>
> Romans 8:26 (NIV)

DAVE

When Gore arrived at Children's, his body temperature was eighty-four degrees. They had spent the last several hours trying to get it back to normal. His temperature was back in the mid-nineties when they made the decision to reverse the course at 2:00 a.m. and pursue the hypothermic treatment. As the name implies, everything about his setting was cold. They ran cold fluids through his tubes, put a cooling blanket underneath him, and placed ice packs on top of him. He looked uncomfortable, and I thought I spotted him shivering.

Amy couldn't stand the thought of him suffering anymore and said, "Dave, he looks like he's in pain. Can't we make him more comfortable?"

"We'll make sure that he's comfortable." Lily looked up and reassured us.

They hooked him up to an EEG machine that required twenty-plus electrodes glued to his head to monitor brain activity during the treatment. Along with this, they put him on a paralytic drug, a painkiller, a sedative, and an antibiotic to fight any possible infection from the water. My heart broke. *It's just so much...so many concerns.*

During the first night, the lights in the room never went off, and our minds raced to the unknown. It was hard to believe that the hospital was investing so many resources into our child who, in all likelihood, was going to die. My heart continuously ached for Amy and Gore. I was immediately concerned about Amy; I knew in addition to the pain we were both experiencing, she had tacked on guilt.

By morning, Gore's targeted body temperature of ninety degrees was reached, and the forty-eight-hour waiting period started. *Will he be able to hold it together and make it through this "experimental" protocol?*

> Trust God from the bottom of your heart;
> don't try to figure out everything on your own.
> Listen for God's voice in everything you do,

everywhere you go; he's the one who will keep you on track.

Proverbs 3:5-6 (The Message)

AMY

I sat in the recliner all night watching Lily, Dr. Jesse, and others attending to Gore. It was then that the last several hours began to take full effect. I was conflicted about what I wanted to know and what I didn't. My mind couldn't clear; I couldn't stop thinking about those few minutes in the cabin.

What was I doing? Had I walked back to the bedroom to get something? Was it two minutes or three minutes that had gone by before I realized he was gone? It was all consuming trying to piece it together.

Shame gnawed at me. I didn't want anybody to know what happened, that I lost my own son. Mom continued calling family and close friends, and each reminder sharply increased the pain. Even though I knew we needed all the prayers, the reality slapped me across the face. I was getting texts from Dave's family on the drive from Gunnison that they were praying for Gore, and it just broke my heart with each new person that heard the news. I knew everyone meant well, but how could I explain to anyone that *I* "lost" our son and that precious, innocent child would pay for it with his life? This nightmare continued to swirl in my head.

Maybe Mary Lynn would know how long it was before we noticed he wasn't in the cabin. What had she seen? I remember her by the ditch.

I needed to hear God's Word, yet my mind was void. It didn't help me when people said, "It's all going to be okay"—that wasn't truth to me at the moment; they didn't *know* he'd be okay.

Although it was late, I called Mary Lynn looking for answers. "I'm sorry. I know it's the middle of the night."

"You know I'm not sleeping. Oh my gosh, Amy, what can I do?"

"I need to know…what were we doing? How long was he missing before we realized it? What was I doing? Was it two minutes? Five?"

"Amy, listen to me. It was two minutes, maybe three at most. We were both right there. I had just checked the latch on the screen door, and it was locked. Don't do this to yourself."

"I can't think of a single scripture. I can't make sense of anything. They gave us a less than one-percent chance…" I whispered almost inaudibly with a lump in my throat. I was barely able to say this aloud.

"I know you, and I *know* you don't want me to sugarcoat anything or say it's gonna be okay. So I'm skipping all of that. I have to tell you what happened earlier tonight, so just try to hear this.

"I was putting all the kids to bed. I was on autopilot and trying to stick with their routine as to not worry them more. They said that you or Dave usually read them a bedtime Bible story, so I told them to pick one out for me to read. Amy, they chose the story of Ezekiel.

"As I read the words in Ezekiel 37, I felt an overwhelming confirmation of God's presence. Ezekiel 37:3 says, 'He asked me, "Son of Man, can these dry bones live?" I said, "O Sovereign Lord, you alone know." …This is what the Sovereign Lord says to these bones: I will make breath enter you, and you will come to life…Then you will know that I am the Lord.'

"Amy, the reason this is so important is because this is *exactly* what I prayed over Gore at the side of the ditch, 'breathe life into these dry bones.' Do you really think that I just randomly prayed that over Gore hours earlier and now here's the same story from a children's Bible book, laid out right in front of me? I didn't choose the story. The kids picked it, and you *know* they can't read. This is God telling us that He is present. He was there the whole time, Amy, and *He* is letting us know that He is right there with you, right now. I know it's hard to hear at this moment, but it's what God led me to say. I'll text you the scripture."

As always, Mary Lynn was unwavering, helping me navigate through the forest of earthly troubles to try to see it God's way. "Thank you. I really need that. Are Kirk and Ryan okay?" I asked wearily.

"They're fine. Don't even worry about them for a second. Your family is amazing—with all your cousins helping me, that's not a concern. I feel like I need to stay here with them for now. I love you."

"I love you. Please don't stop praying."

"I promise." We hung up.

There it was—that phenomenon that kept us hanging on to hope. Every time that I felt that I wasn't going to make it to the next minute, someone told a story like this one of how obvious God's presence was, or they sent a verse that spoke so clearly to us.

People were praying for this child—even people who normally didn't pray. We received messages from others that we didn't even know; friends shared with us about their church or school or town that was praying for Gore. It was the body of Christ like we had never experienced before.

And there was something else. There were a few times when I had prayed so exhaustively that I could pray no more. At the same time, there were relatives and friends whose faith had been weak or wavering. Now, they had thrown themselves into Gore's fight as if it were their own. They had prayed so fervently and believed for us when we simply did not have the strength. A strange thought process began to evolve, but it made sense at the time. *Are we going to have to give up Gore to bring about something life changing for someone else?* These thoughts were both comforting and excruciating.

> Therefore I endure everything for the sake of the elect, that they too may obtain the *salvation* that is in Christ Jesus, with eternal glory.
>
> 2 Timothy 2:10 (NIV)

Hanging On:
Wednesday

Amy

Morning broke, and I was hanging on. At 5:00 a.m., they had to change out some IVs on Gore. They had put tiny lines in for the IV when they didn't think there was any hope, and it was difficult for Lily to pull blood from them as often as they needed for monitoring purposes during the hypothermic protocol. The decision was made that Dr. Jesse would sew two larger lines into his femoral vein and artery. Then it became a routine of drawing blood, checking his Foley to make sure his kidneys were functioning and that he was urinating, checking his diapers to see if his bowels were working, and checking all his blood work around the clock to see if his pH level was normalizing. The simple explanation given to us at the time was that Gore's pH had dropped to a dangerous level. Because of the extended amount of time without oxygen, cell death had occurred. As a result, acid accumulated in his blood and tissues (also referred to as acidosis).

My mom had called my sister, Anne, the night before, and she was getting the first flight out of Dallas. She was there first thing Wednesday morning. The door swung open. Anne rushed in, blonde hair swept back in a messy ponytail, blue eyes wide.

"Amy!" she called through tears. We were both speechless and hugged one another tightly. Anne arched her head over and saw Gore, causing a fresh onslaught of tears. We had always been very close, talked on the phone several times a week, and visited every chance we could. I knew she felt my pain as well as anyone could.

"You're going to get through this, Amy," she reassured me in spite of our despair.

It was almost impossible to feel comfort in this situation, but Anne surrounded me with her warm, loving presence. We always laughed that she was much sweeter than I, a gentler spirit, kindhearted, and soft spoken. I felt relieved that she had arrived.

"You have to start thinking about Kirk and Ryan. They need you, so you're going to have to be strong for *them*. They need their mom," she said, trying to keep from breaking down.

Somewhere in the midst of her reminder, I laid my head down on her lap and cried. She has three beautiful children of her own, so she shared my deepest fears. It's innate. You don't have to dig deep to find the empathy—if you are a mother and you witness another mother hurting regarding their child, you understand. This was her nephew that she loved like her own. Just last summer, she was instructing me that I needed to

"let my boys be boys and stop being so overprotective."
Well, I was trying.

———◆———

Our phones lit up and buzzed nonstop. Between
our friends, families, church groups, prayer chains,
and Facebook, the word had spread. Dave would call
someone in his family to give an update, they would pass
news along, and my parents kept our side informed. We
also experienced a constant stream of visitors; we were
truly blessed with an extensive support system.

Dave and I talked only a little bit, but we both
agreed that we would take anything. We just wanted
him to live. We weren't yet processing quality of life,
just life itself.

Wednesday was the day that we met our nurses,
Corrie and Laura. Silence dominated the atmosphere
that day, but I was drawn to them and knew Gore was
in skillful hands. Corrie had blonde hair, a big smile,
and piercing blue eyes that focused when she listened.
She looked "in charge" and secure as I gathered she was
training Laura. Not only did they monitor Gore but us
as well.

"Have you two even slept? I *know* you haven't
eaten anything, but you obviously don't need any more
coffee," Corrie said lightheartedly as she scanned the
ledge filled from one end to the other with coffee cups.
It's part of what makes the nurses so good—they have
to manage us almost as much as the patient.

When my sister, Anne, walked in, Corrie grinned.
Later she said, "I don't know if your sister brought

enough clothes in that suitcase. She looks like she's ready for a month-long vacation."

In spite of myself, I smiled. "She came from Texas and didn't have anywhere to put her bags. She came straight here." Even with the explanation, I knew Corrie was just teasing to try and lift our spirits.

In the weary hours of the day, we would stare intently at the EEG screen or quietly talk to Gore. Feeling so sure that he was aware of me, I would cover him up with a blanket, but Corrie would come in and take it off. I envisioned him back in his comfy bed with his blanket, surrounded by his stuffed animal cronies, and *so* wanted our life as it was before. Closing my eyes wistfully, I would've given anything in the world to have Gore wake me up at two thirty in the morning again and to feel his breath on my face.

While lost in these fantasies of mine, Dave tried to draw me out with silly comments like, "I think when he wakes up, we shouldn't give him his binky back. He'll never know."

I rolled my eyes and said, "If this kid wakes up, he can have *anything* he wants."

My mind moved to Ryan. *Oh, she is going to be devastated. She loves her little brothers like nothing I've ever seen. How would I explain this to her? All the joy that this child brings her…*

I couldn't even run through the conversation in my head. At age five, Ryan would have done anything for her Goresky. She wouldn't understand why she had to give him up.

The day was a blur. A few friends from our church had come to pray with us. I could hear their prayers, but I felt lost. My head knew it was what we needed, but I did *not* want to hear comforting words. I wanted to scream.

I wildly thought of scenes from the accident while listening to those around me trying to work out the timeline of the previous night's events. My mind was swimming, and all I could do was stare at Gore and think about his last minutes in the water. *Did he know? Did he know that we were doing everything to find him? Is he with Jesus so he doesn't have to suffer anymore?* From the looks of his flat line EEG, he wasn't there with us.

I want him back! I don't want to feel this staggering pain on his birthday or celebrate Christmas without him. I need to rewind the last twelve hours of our lives and redo them. That's what I want. I want a do over. Lord, help me try to understand this. I am so afraid.

At that moment, I realized that being a Christian wasn't making the pain and suffering easier. It was excruciating, but at the end of whatever was about to happen, Dave and I needed to try to arrive at a place of peace knowing Gore was in God's hands…and He may *not* save him.

"You're the Ancient of Days," I prayed. "Even if I don't understand Your plan, You're all I have. And I *have* to trust that You are who You say You are."

> Our task is not to decipher exactly how all of life's pieces fit and what they all mean but to remain faithful and obedient to God, who knows all mysteries. That is the kind of faith that

is pleasing to God—a faith that is determined to trust him when he has not answered all the questions, when we have not heard the voice from the whirlwind.

Nancy Guthrie's *Holding Onto Hope*

Dave

When the "cooling" procedure began, the doctors hooked Gore up to an EEG machine to ensure he wasn't having seizures. If he had any, they would abort the treatment. We stared at that screen looking for any tiny little "blip" or "peak" to rise on *any* line. Ironically, we would study it endlessly as if we were doctors or people that could accurately read it, but then gave it little credibility. It wasn't until later that we realized how silly we must've looked staring at it, holding our coffee, pointing at the screen that looked the same as it had the entire time.

Each day, Dr. Carpenter, the attending physician, would come in our room and say, "We'd like to see more going on here," as he pointed to the EEG screen.

"Yes, but he is 'frozen' and paralyzed and on a painkiller *and* a sedative. What can we expect?" said Amy.

"You're right. We don't really know," said Dr. Carpenter as casually as he could muster. Part of me thinks that they didn't really know since they didn't have a lot of research in these situations, and part of me thinks that he just let us live in our own little world, powered by the smallest rays of hope. Whatever it was,

I felt a sincere empathy from him when he spoke these words. It's God's grace that didn't allow us to have any idea how bad that EEG really looked. Despite the small squiggly lines, it was flat lined.

Mary Lynn had insisted upon staying in Gunnison and taking care of four kids and our Lab, Wylie. My cousins helped her in keeping Kirk and Ryan blissfully unaware and occupied back at Jennings.

"Look at us—late-night movies!" She texted Amy a picture of Kirk and Ryan, snuggled in a comforter, eating popcorn. We also received a picture with messily painted words, saying, "Love, Hope, Faith–To: Gore From: Ryan." Our spirits rose seeing this; I knew the kids were entertained (and being spoiled rotten), so that put us at ease. They explained that Kirk and Ryan hadn't seen anything the night of the accident but had heard the ambulance. They were told Gore was hurt but he was trying to get better.

As all their fun and games progressed, Gore lay still and quiet.

"Gore," I called. Examining his body, I tried to find a patch of skin that wasn't covered in wires and equipment. It was hard to not hold him, and he was freezing to the touch. I thought wishfully, *It's as if he is just waiting for something...*

We were waiting for something too. It had been a long and intense day of observing Gore while he lay motionless and cold, and we were left with our own contemplation. We were completely powerless. The prognosis was grim, and all we had to do was wait and see if this cooling treatment that they "didn't think would make any difference" would do anything for Gore. In the middle of the night, we tried to steal sporadic rest amidst all the thoughts swirling in our minds.

Deep personal questions circled through my mind all day. Each time I left Gore's room to wander to the bathroom, get a cup of coffee, or just roam around aimlessly, I would cry.

What will tomorrow bring? What if Gore never wakes up? When I was first blindsided with the news, all I wanted was to be able to hold Gore again. He is alive, but I haven't been able to hold him. Does that count? Is it just the machines that are keeping him alive?

I am scared for my family and my wife. What kind of marriage will we have? How will Kirk and Ryan be able to get past this? I am scared for the deep scars that Amy will carry with her forever. We talked before about how difficult it would be for any family to overcome the loss of a child. Could we?

What if Gore is brain dead? What kind of decisions are we going to have to make?

Will we ever go back to Jennings or Gunnison? Will the rest of the family?

I can step up my game and take this lesson to be a better man, a better husband, and a better dad. Why God? Tell me. What are You trying to show me?

Give me peace because I have zero right now. Give Amy peace. Amy is the strongest person I know, but will she be strong enough to forgive herself?

Are you hearing me, God?

> And the God of all grace, who called you to his eternal glory in Christ, after you have suffered

a little while, will himself restore you and make
you strong, firm and steadfast.

1 Peter 5:10 (NIV)

AMY

In the midst of our valley, when we were in survival
mode and hanging on by a thread, God sent us someone.

I allowed myself to see this on Wednesday night.
The nurses switched at 6:45 p.m. Sluggishly, I tilted
my head to the door. Two nurses escorted a blond, curly
haired boy into the room.

"This is your nurse for the night, Lukas," said Corrie,
smiling as if she knew a secret.

*There is no way he is old enough to be caring for our son.
Do they not see how sick our child is? He must be twenty at
best.* It turned out that he was twenty-six, but it didn't
matter. I quickly ate my negative thoughts. Lukas went
to work, and almost immediately Dave and I connected
with him. We quickly realized he was a Christian and
were thankful that he felt comfortable to talk about it.

Lukas's demeanor was instantly calming. He listened
intently as we voiced any concerns or thoughts we
were having and very clearly explained and answered
our questions.

A little while later, when he began to change Gore's
diaper, I said, "Oh, I'll do that."

He gently replied, "It's okay. It's part of my job."

My eyes welled up, and I asked again. "Please. Let
me do it. I want to."

He must have sensed my need to change Gore's diaper for fear I wouldn't change many more. Moving aside, he let me step in.

After several dirty diaper changes, I asked, "Why is he doing this?" Lukas explained that because of the lack of oxygen, cell death had occurred, and this was the result: the sloughing off of everything in his stomach. It was to be expected. I knew this wasn't a good sign.

Again that night, the news wasn't great.

"Gore's not peeing," Lukas said, furrowing his brow in concentration.

Immediately, I thought, *Oh no. His kidneys are shutting down.*

Lukas saw my lip begin to quiver and patted me on the shoulder. "Don't worry. We might be able to correct this." He whipped out a large syringe that made my head spin. "I think the catheter is clogged," he clarified. Syringe after syringe of urine was extracted. Lukas promptly fixed this issue, thankfully eradicating another concern.

My appraisal of Lukas had been completely unfair. I later told Dave, "This is a gift. God knew that we needed this consolation."

After attempting to sleep a few hours, I woke up about 1:00 a.m. and started talking to Lukas again. I felt drawn to his calm demeanor and gravitated to Gore's bedside. Just like Lily the night before, he always seemed to be in our room, constantly attentive to Gore.

Soon, we were in deep conversation about CPR—how my dad and cousins were on the scene using their medical professionalism to resuscitate Gore. Lukas affirmed how important it was that Gore received this quality CPR.

"I just couldn't be more thankful that they were around. They shoved aside their emotions and did everything they could," I said.

"You do what you gotta do in those situations," said Lukas. "The irony is that doctors never want family nearby in these emergency situations. They cause distress and distract from the emergency at hand. Your dad was pitted in the scene as a family member and a doctor—two roles that can't usually coexist successfully in such an emotional situation."

I couldn't imagine taking on that task and separating the two roles. "Even in the back of the ambulance, I didn't think it had made any difference, but I knew they all tried in the midst of their own pain."

Lukas sat thoughtfully for a moment and then said, "I wonder if that's why your dad went to medical school." Wow, that struck me as extremely profound and insightful.

I found myself talking to Lukas but quickly realized that it was a rather one-sided conversation. It was simply a running stream of consciousness that he undeservedly got the brunt of.

"I know God has the power to save him, but I'm not sure that's what's going to happen here... I never thought I would have to face something like this."

Lukas understood I was processing and would listen quietly as if he were letting me get to where I was going on my own. "I don't know if I can do this, Lukas. Can I make it through with my faith intact? I don't know anything else. I know God is sovereign. I have always said that no matter what, I don't want to try to live my life without Him. I would fail so miserably. I fail every day with God. Imagine me without Him. It would not be pretty."

Lukas nodded or asked me a question that only spiraled me back into running at the mouth. "I have to decide now that no matter what happens, God is still the same God, and He is going to be sitting on His throne. I have to know that we can get through this…."

Walking away from God would be catastrophic. The only thing worse than losing my child would be losing my child and my faith.

Everything was colliding; everything I had known to be true and believed in for so long was hanging in the balance. But even if my words seemed more for my own convincing, I clung to God.

After a few hours, Lukas enthusiastically announced some great news. "Gore has a pupil response!"

Dave and I flew to Gore's bedside at once.

"Really? Let me see!" I took the flashlight and attempted to examine Gore's eyes myself. Next, Lukas wanted to run a small test on Gore. He needed to see if Gore would move if the drugs that were keeping him motionless were turned off. About an hour and a half after Lukas had turned down his paralytic, Gore moved the slightest bit. It seems tiny, but these were two monumental things that gave us some hope. It was a "good" night, and we felt better on Thursday morning when the sun came up.

> It's in Christ that we find out who we are and what we are living for. Long before we first heard of Christ and got our hopes up, he had his eye on us, had designs on us for glorious living, part of the overall purpose he is working out in everything and everyone.
>
> Ephesians 1:11-12 (The Message)

Believing God:
Thursday

Dave

The good feeling didn't last long.

One of the doctors walked in the room, and Amy and I jumped up. "We saw a pupil response!" we said almost in unison, eager to share this step forward.

But this step forward became two steps backward quickly.

The doctor shook his head. "That's just basic brain-stem function," he said.

"What does that mean?"

Here came the bombshell: "Basic brain stem function can keep him alive. But that doesn't mean that there is anything *going on* in his brain, if that makes sense."

That sank us quickly. Yes, the doctors were being honest, and he had every right to say that based on all we knew, but we were crushed. We understood and knew it was bad, but we couldn't start thinking about having to make decisions on quality of life. *Couldn't* and didn't have room for that in our minds.

That morning, we began to come out of our shock and attempted to be more present than we had been on Wednesday. Since Amy and I were only sleeping random hours of the night, we were up and had several cups of coffee when it was time for Lukas to leave and for Corrie and Laura to take over the day shift.

As Corrie and Laura walked in, Lukas was ready to share all the information that he had gleaned from us on Wednesday night.

"Good morning, Corrie. Did you know that Dave attended the same college as you in Washington?" said Lukas facetiously.

"I do because you texted me last night to inform me," replied Corrie.

"Oh, did I also mention that Dave and Amy are involved with *YoungLife* like your brother?" Lukas said as if he were working toward something.

"Yes, you did text me that last night too," Corrie said. She continued to play along. "What other great things did you do that you wanna share?"

"Oh, did I put in my text that *I* cleared Gore's Foley and his kidneys seem to be fine?"

"Yes, Lukas. You clearly did mention that in your text titled *Facts That I Learned about the Ottesons Tonight That You Should Know*. I'm so proud of you. Did I mention to you that yesterday was crazy and Amy wasn't exactly chatting it up with *anyone*?"

She turned toward us with a goofy look, and we all started to laugh; that laugh was my first since Tuesday. Enjoying the friendly competition, I felt reassured that Gore was on their minds even when one of them wasn't there. Corrie and Lukas were close, and their goals and perspectives matched perfectly. They were doing everything in their power to help Gore as his nurses, and they had faith in something much bigger than themselves. That was paramount for us at the time.

The added bonus was that they did a great job of attempting to lift our spirits and giving us rays of hope. I never felt that they gave us *false* hope, but their demeanor was uplifting despite the grave circumstances.

❖

"We know God has the ability to save Gore. We just don't know if He will," I asserted after hours of reflection. "We don't know *why* all this happened."

Corrie paused what she was doing and looked directly at me. "In almost eight years of nursing in the PICU, I don't think I've ever heard any parent not only say that but also say it with complete abandon. I believe you and Amy when you say it," she said. "I was worried about how you two were coping, but I realize you *get it*. You truly know that He can, *and He may not*, but that wouldn't change who He is to you. That's a hard place to arrive."

We understood the magnitude of Gore's injuries, but we were also trying to see them through a lens of faith and trust in God. Corrie had to assess where we were in regards to making hard decisions should God choose against healing Gore completely. Corrie's faith gave her a unique perspective in light of never-ending sadness in the PICU. She had seen plenty of death and pain, not only in the children that she cared for but for their entire families.

I sat in Gore's room, thinking, *What if Amy and I didn't believe that Gore was going to be in heaven? I have the hope that God can save him, but we may have to open up our hand and let him go. God knows exactly what will happen next; that's what we can hope in.* If I hadn't continuously circulated that thought in my mind, I would've gone crazy.

———◈———

People from all around us started praying for miracles—generally for healing Gore and peace and strength for Amy and me. More specifically, we witnessed people praying for things such as "complete healing," his eyesight, his hearing, healing for his organs, a smile for his mouth, and so on. These weren't just token prayers; these came from close friends and family and other prayer warriors we didn't even know who *sincerely* believed their prayers could be answered. We knew that complete healing was not something that we were given any reason to hope in, but nevertheless, we continued to hope.

> If you don't know what you're doing, pray to the Father. He loves to help. You'll get his help, and won't be condescended to when you ask for it. Ask boldly, believingly, without a second thought. People who "worry their prayers" are like wind-whipped waves. Don't think you're going to get anything from the Master that way, adrift at sea, keeping all your options open.
>
> James 1: 5-8 (The Message)

A̲MY

My parents came to Gore's room first thing Thursday morning. Mom announced, "I brought something from Gore's room at home." It was a frame that said *Miracle* across the bottom that he received as a gift when he was born. I had always kept a picture of him in it. My mom said with conviction, "I think we need this in here." It was a reminder that although everything was so uncertain, our son wasn't dead. He was still fighting.

To our heartache, we were apart from Kirk and Ryan. Mom brought pictures of them too, so we taped pictures of all three kids to the wall so we could see them all day. Gore's body was also swelling, and I wanted people to be able to see what he really looked like—the blond, pink-cheeked child with the jester smile. The nurses said the swelling was normal, but we had to hope his brain wasn't swelling.

I found my mind constantly wandering to a Bible study that I had done called *Believing God* by Beth Moore; it kept popping into my head. I didn't realize until much later that it had been almost five years since I had done that study, but it was as if it were only a few months prior. Thoughts and statements that had made a profound impact on me during the study were resurfacing.

Think, Amy. What was it that God taught me and wants me to hear right now? There were five statements at the beginning of the study that were referenced at the start of every lesson. I found myself recycling the first two over and over.

1. God is who He says He is, and

2. God can do what He says He can do.

In chapter one, Beth discusses Ephesians 1:19-20. In reference to those verses, Beth says, "God exerts incomparable power in the lives of those who continue believing Him." She then goes on to say,

> Can you think of any need you might have that would require more strength than God exercised to raise the dead? Me neither. God can raise marriages from the dead, and He can restore life and purpose to those who have given up. He can forgive and purify the vilest sinner. You have *no* need that exceeds His power.[1]

Wow! We have a need, God. We need you to raise our son up.

There were many thoughts that ran through my head regarding this study, but I became very focused on one thing: we sell God short. We ask Him for too little. We act as if He can't handle what we need (I'm guilty). We had been praying for anything—for Gore to have *any* quality of life. At first, our prayer was, "We will take anything, God, just let him live." I was mad at myself for lacking the faith to pray more boldly after my mind had drifted to the quality of life thoughts.

I thought, *What are we doing? We are selling God short. We are asking Him for so little when there is "No need that exceeds His power."* It was time to start believing God. We started asking everyone, "Pray for a miracle." Truly, that is what we needed to be praying, but we also needed to have utmost belief too. God could do it. It might not be His will, but we had to at least ask.

Even if Gore didn't wake up, I have to trust in God's goodness. If I lost my faith, I'd have nothing. I imagined parents who suffered the worst possible pain of a child's death. Their desolation must be incomparably profound if they thought that was the actual end or that God wasn't in control. How could we continue without trusting in God's infinite wisdom? My faith is my anchor, and I wasn't going to believe only when it was convenient. Comprehending God's plan is impossible for finite beings. I reminded myself that attempting to understand his omniscient perspective would be like our dog attempting calculus. As mysterious as life can be, I reminded myself of God's infinite wisdom and my life in comparison—it was a mere flicker of light in the history of time.

> I also pray that you will understand the incredible greatness of God's power for us who believe him. This is the same mighty power that raised Christ from the dead and seated him in the place of honor at God's right hand in the heavenly realms.
>
> Ephesians 1:19-20 (NLT)

Laurie holding Amy right after she fell in
the irrigation ditch many years ago.

Gore, Dave and Amy on July 4, 2010 – two days before
the accident. See the orange fencing in the background.

Looking toward the cabin on the Fourth of July
with the temporary fencing in the foreground.

The ditch

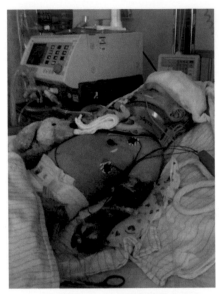

Gore in the PICU.

Coach and Gore when he was first holding his head up.

Ryan's painting for Gore.

Gore in his special chair on the rehabilitation
floor with no expression.

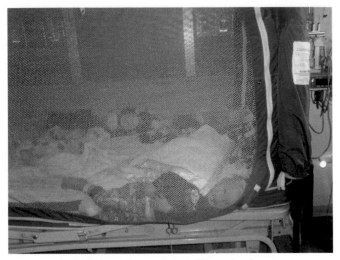

Gore playing in his Posey bed.

Kirk, Ryan, and Gore together at one
of Gore's PT/OT sessions.

Dr. Oleszek keeping Gore steady while
Gretchen, Gore's PT, watches.

Gore's first steps.

Gore and Granddad Kirk when he was
just getting his smile back.

Gore with Corrie and Lukas a few days
before we left the hospital.

Our family the day we arrived home.

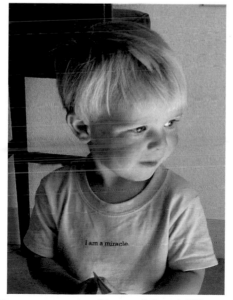

Gore wearing his "I am a Miracle" T-shirt.

Gore at the cross by the ditch.

Gore and his granddad exactly one year later: July 6, 2011.

Amy and Mary Lynn

Gore back to normal (Photo by Jennifer Johnson)

Gore, Kirk, and Ryan on the front porch of the cabin.

THE BREAKDOWN

AMY

Beginning with the doctor's explanation of pupil reaction being nothing more significant than basic brainstem function, Thursday was a rollercoaster. We started asking people *not* to visit, simply because we were exhausted and had already broken the PICU rules numerous times by exceeding the maximum number of visitors.

"We appreciate the support," Dave managed, "but we know everyone is doing the best thing they can do, and that is to pray."

Later that day, Dave informed me, "Doug is coming from Seattle," referring to his identical twin.

"I'm glad," I said. I *really* was. Dave was going to need someone there for him, and I wasn't much support. I knew he had been going outside to collect himself before he unfailingly put on his mask of strength when he rejoined me.

When Doug finally arrived, I excused myself so they could be alone. Joining my family to try to eat, I felt restless. I wasn't hungry and didn't want to be in a cafeteria full of people.

There I was, thinking about our son, the flat line, and the emptiness on his face.

Maddening thoughts flashed across my mind: *What if he doesn't make it? What if this is prolonging the inevitable?*

Thinking again about Gore, our vent-hoarding, Hershey-stealing, "nake-dancing," smile-flashing son…now so still. Lifeless.

His tiny body on the ditch bank.

The pale cheeks…woefully pale cheeks.

And I felt like it was completely my fault.

Instability inflated deep inside me, rising to fill my chest. I knew my head wasn't right.

"Excuse me," I abruptly said, pushing the chair away from the table. Mom and Dad looked at me surprised but didn't try to stop me. I quickly exited the cafeteria and lunged toward the doors of the main entrance. A breakdown bubbled within me. I started quickly walking as far away from the hospital as I could get before I allowed the meltdown to begin. My pace quickened to a run.

Suddenly everything was coming to a head. All the emotion that I had shoved deep inside was about to peak and spill out in an ugly cry. It was bottled up, and I knew that I had to release it. The tears fell. I heard myself crying and was storming around some random parking lot a few blocks from the hospital—luckily empty. I was alone with God. Hardly able to stand under the guilt I felt, I knew I needed to be present for what was happening at that moment and in the hours to come.

"Please, God," I begged, "I *need* some kind of understanding for what's taking place." The tears felt like acid stinging my eyes. Distractedly pacing the lot, I knew I just needed to work it out with God.

Right then, those elusive words flashed through my mind as an epiphany. God had been preparing me. The words from the *Believing God* study rang in my ears: "*Forgive me for my unbelief.* I know I say I believe, but my unbelief is my sin. I need to trust You." Although I said God has a plan and God is sovereign, I was terrified. I wanted answers, but what I really needed was to wait for God's time and seek his forgiveness for my inability to trust Him with *every* fiber of my being during this tumultuous time.

I began reflecting on my relationship with Christ. Even during times when my life seemed off track, I never doubted His faithfulness. He never left me. 2 Timothy 2:13 says: "If we are faithless, he will remain faithful, for he cannot disown himself."

At that moment, I knew what I needed to do. I had to ask for it *all*.

Sitting down on the pavement, I clasped my hands together. "God, I want complete healing. You tell us we can ask for big things, so I'm asking right now. I want *total and complete* healing. I want the same little boy I knew on July 6—no more of this 'I'll take anything' stuff. I want *You* to get *all* the glory."

Our human minds could grasp the severity of the damage that had been done to Gore's brain.

Well, I wanted God to intercede and defy *every* odd, statistic, and percentage that we had been given. It was undoubtedly within His power.

Show us your omnipotence, Lord. It was one of those moments that I will never forget for the rest of my life. I began to feel an overwhelming peace; I began to feel that God met me in that parking lot.

He never said it was going to be fine.

He never said that He was going to heal our son; that was certainly not the message.

There was never an audible voice, but I felt the presence of God like I had never experienced in my life. He heard my prayer of surrender. The peace unfolding in my heart told me that He was sovereign and in control of everything—no matter the outcome.

What I realized at that moment was that I didn't want to be in the way of God's plan. Yes, I wanted our son to be whole. Like any parent whose child is in some catastrophic accident or living through years of cancer and pain, we want complete healing. We can't control the outcome. But we *can* control how we respond to the situation.

God, my role is to believe You, no matter what. You are who You say You are. You can do what You say You can do.

> Let us hold unswervingly to the hope we profess, for he who promised is faithful.
>
> Hebrews 10:23 (NIV)

DAVE

When Amy went downstairs with her family, I felt relieved. I needed to ask Corrie some difficult questions that I didn't want Amy to hear. I needed more concrete answers—anything to start processing. By nature, I'm a fixer. Often Amy would tell me, "Please don't try to fix this. Just let me be sad or mad for a little while." She and I would have to process all of this in our own way, but the waiting was becoming more than I could take. After discussing this with Doug, I bolstered up my nerves when Corrie walked in.

"Corrie, I need you to tell me the truth," I said, hearing my voice catch. Corrie's eyes widened as if she knew where I was headed. "How many cases have you seen like this, and what was the outcome?"

Corrie's look said it all. She had always been forthright with us, but now she seemed to be searching for the right words. "Dave, I have seen a lot of drowning cases. I wish I could tell you they have good outcomes. I have never seen a child who was down as long as Gore. I'm sorry. We just have to wait and see."

My mind raced again; I didn't hear much after that.

Now I knew. It was time to prepare myself for the worst.

Amy quietly closed the door as she entered Gore's room. I couldn't help but notice a wave of calm settled over her; her eyes reflected serenity instead of devastation for the first time in two days. She scanned the room to see who was present. She asked Anne, "Will you stay with Gore for a little bit? I need to talk to Dave."

Anne nodded. I could tell something had happened, but Amy seemed more excited than distressed. Curious, I hurried to join her.

We left the room for the first time together. Walking to a bench in the hospital garden, Amy began to discuss her experience. Her words spoke to me and I began to process what Amy felt she heard God say: "I am who I say I am and I am in complete control, no matter what." As I felt the warm sun on my face, I began thinking about Colorado's winters, I recalled the pounding of snow we were subject to, particularly in Gunnison. The beauty and warmth we were currently experiencing seemed so faraway, so unlikely then. But God shapes beauty from the wreckage of winter. And the same concept applies to life.

We prayed together for a while. We prayed for total healing for Gore, for peace, for our lack of faith, and for strength to handle whatever would happen tomorrow when they would warm Gore up. I can honestly say we both walked away from that bench with a huge weight lifted from our souls.

Entering Gore's room, our fortified sense of faith surged through me. I sat beside his bed, looking at his tiny frame that was surrounded and penetrated by equipment and wires. *We are going to get through this*. I was certain.

"I get it now, Gore," said Amy. She began to softly speak to him while stroking his little white hand. "God loves you more than we do. I believe it with all my heart. Our children aren't ours. You're a gift." In that moment, I was so proud of Amy. This acknowledgment was huge for her, the "overprotector," and a witness to her trust in the Lord.

It was time for the nurses to change shifts again. Corrie and Lukas exchanged their usual pleasantries and gave us comic relief. Corrie explained what to expect in the morning when she returned.

"You're headed into the homestretch of the hypothermic treatment. We're going to begin warming him back to his regular temperature, and then we'll turn the paralytic off to see what happens next," said Corrie. "We'll remove the cold fluids and take away the ice packs and cooling blanket, but we have to do all this slowly. It will take time. He's done well through the entire treatment. But we need a movement that tells us he's in there and can feel things or hear things and move in response to them."

That night, Mary Lynn sent Amy a text regarding the story of Lazarus in John 11. This is the story of Mary and Martha and their brother, Lazarus, who dies. Mary Lynn's text said, "Mary and Martha are 'put out' with Jesus that he waited so long to come. When Jesus arrives, Lazarus has been dead for four days but rises up when Jesus commands. Jesus then says to Mary and Martha, 'Did I not tell you that if you believed, you would see the glory of God?'" (v. 40).

Mary Lynn went on to say, "It *has* to be like this so God gets all the glory. It's evident that there's nothing else medically possible that can be done, and now the outcome could *only* point to the healing power of Jesus. We have to wait on God."

Wow! It blew us both away. We were edified and on the same page with Mary Lynn's rich understanding. We knew that medically everything had been done for Gore. Everyone from those first moments until now had fought so hard and pressed the limits of medicine to aid Gore's recovery. Now we had to wait for God's plan to unfold.

> Your ways, O God, are holy. What god is so great as our God? You are the God who performs miracles; you display your power among the peoples.
>
> Psalm 77:13-14 (NIV)

Part Three:
The Miraculous Return

THE AWAKENING: FRIDAY

AMY

Dave and I had dozed off, and I woke up some time in the middle of the night hearing Lukas with Gore. I rose and sleepily shuffled to Gore's bed.

"I turned the paralytic down again two hours ago to test for any movement," said Lukas.

I watched Gore closely, waiting and hoping.

Suddenly, Gore reached up with his right arm toward the tube from the ventilator. Lukas quickly grabbed his arm and held it so he couldn't get to it. As soon as he did this, Gore then raised his left arm. I grabbed that one. *What just happened?* I looked at Lukas, stunned, but then the biggest grin splashed across my face. Lukas quickly turned the paralytic and sedative back up; we didn't want him to be uncomfortable and *definitely* didn't want him to pull his tube out. Unable to hide my ecstasy, I immediately woke Dave up to tell him.

"I know this may seem small…I know he could still have severe brain damage, but this is hope," I said.

The night transitioned into a bright-orange dawn. We were ready for what the day ahead would hold. Dave and I began the day reading John 11 and the story of Lazarus.

"Did I not tell you that if you believed, you would see the glory of God?"

"It had to be this way so that God gets all the glory."

Those verses, along with Mary Lynn's texts, exemplify everything that happened that day. They were branded in my mind.

The doctors told us everything was going as planned, but they were going to warm up Gore earlier than expected. *This is getting better*, we thought. A doctor by the name of Daya had been in several times the last few days. His demeanor was quiet yet genuine. When Dr. Daya walked in early that morning, he was smiling and had his hands in his pockets. He walked over, stood across the bed quietly for a minute, then looked at me, and said, "It's going to be a good day."

What made him say that? It struck me as a very encouraging thing to say on a day that most seemed to believe was going to be anything but positive. Did he feel God's presence in the room? It stays with me to this day.

I was beaming. "It *is* going to be a good day, Dr. Daya. It is."

And so it began.

———◆———

Warming Gore back to his normal temperature was a gradual process. The key waiting moments were before us. Gore had given response after only a couple hours, when Lukas had "tested" him the prior nights. So we had hope that if anything was going to happen, it would be within the next two hours. Back to the waiting, hoping, watching, and praying.

"Still nothing," I murmured, resting my head against Dave. His face was impassive but still lit with expectancy.

All day we stared at that EEG computer screen. Nothing was happening. He was getting warm, but there wasn't any more brain activity than there had been for the last forty-eight hours. We also knew that they had turned the paralytic off, and it didn't appear to make a difference.

Suddenly, Corrie made a call to the technician. I was shocked at what I heard: "Yeah, go ahead and come take the EEG off."

"Wait, what's going on?" I asked alarmed.

"We don't need it. Gore is warm, and we only needed to monitor for seizures during the protocol. That's over. It needs to go."

All my reasons for the EEG's flat lines during the past forty-eight hours were being rectified. He was no longer cold or sedated. I was running out of things to blame for what appeared to be little "amplitude" (a term we had heard way too often). Why wasn't that monitor reflecting more brain activity? The medical explanations weren't exactly clear to me, but it didn't matter because my mind began to race toward a horrible possibility that I hadn't allowed until this moment.

If he's brain dead, what decisions are we about to face? I had been so focused on Gore living that I hadn't thought about making excruciating decisions about Gore's quality of life, his organs, or where we would bury him. Dave and I hadn't discussed any of it. *Is Dave thinking about these things?*

My mind played back the comments from the doctors: "That's just basic brain stem function," or, "his organs should begin to shut down." But what if they hadn't? What if his brain is severely damaged but not other organs?

For me, my body on earth is merely a vessel. Therefore, I've always been a believer of organ donation, and Dave and I set up a living will with instructions on what to do with our bodies. I've never wanted to be buried, always telling Dave that I want anything that could be salvaged and used for good to be used.

That thought roamed around my head, but it was a totally different thought process when it came to our child. Several very bad things must occur in order to trigger a notification to the nurses that Donor Alliance must be contacted. This was the case with Gore. Obviously, this was not something they announced to us, but Donor Alliance was discreetly waiting on the floor that day in anticipation of Gore's outcome.

God, give us the strength we need to move on if Gore is…Gore is…brain dead. I knew that if we were going to lose Gore, I wanted another child to be helped. It was the only thing that could comfort me about the entire topic. Good had to come out of this.

Don't let us hang on to him just to be kept alive on machines. That was as far as I could travel down *that* road. *Give us strength to let Gore go if he's not going to have any quality of life. Let him help another child.*

> Be joyful in hope, patient in affliction, faithful in prayer.
>
> Romans 12:12 (NIV)

DAVE

Amy and I spent much time over his bed together, watching and waiting. At the hour mark, Gore wasn't moving at all. At the one-and-a-half-hour mark, Gore wasn't moving at all. Then we got to the two-hour mark and small "what if?" questions started circling our minds. Not many words were spoken between us. Suspense permeated the room.

"C'mon, Gore, do you want to wake up?"

No response.

"Gore, can you hear me?"

No movement.

Okay, two and a half hours. "Hi, Gore, do you want to wake up?"

Nothing.

What in the world?

"I'm texting Mary Lynn that nothing's happening," said Amy stoically. Almost instantly, Mary Lynn replied in reference to our Lazarus story.

"Okay. So you are Mary and Martha, and you wait."

Waiting was easier said than done. At this point, Dr. Carpenter came in and said, "Shut it all down. Turn off his sedative and his pain meds as well. We should be seeing something by now."

"We haven't talked at all about what we're going to do if he is brain dead," I whispered regarding the chilling realization.

"I can't talk about that right now," was all Amy said while keeping her eyes fixated on Gore. I agreed wholeheartedly, and it was never spoken of again.

We surpassed the three-hour mark, and deep concern started to sweep over us as we looked blankly at each other. How could he have had responses before and nothing was happening now?

There was also the MRI question. If Gore woke up, this was the next step in order to assess the damage. But every time we asked about it, we received different answers.

"Oh, we probably won't need that *today...*"

"Maybe later this evening."

"This afternoon?"

No one's giving me a straight answer. Attempting to dispel my fear, I sensed they weren't pushing for the MRI because they didn't think there would be a need for one.

Three and a half hours later—*is that stirring?*

"Amy!" my voice cracked as I reached for her before recognizing she had been there the whole time, also on the edge of her seat.

Gore looked as if his smallest muscles were shot with a volt of electricity and reconnecting to produce the tiniest movements: a clench here, a twitch there. His larger muscles were then reined in. Stirring increased.

We now couldn't leave him alone.

"Oh, guys, I *know* you want to be all over him and hurry him up. But we have to let him take his time," Corrie reminded us. She had to tell us this about five more times before she outright said, "Stop poking and touching him!" In spite of this, her body leaned toward Gore fully engrossed too, and she never unglued her eyes from his bed even while kindly reprimanding us.

Finally, the electric current that we could see running through our boy crept to his eyes. The lids struggled for a moment, then—

"Thank you, Lord!" Amy jumped up, and my face cracked in half with a grin.

Gore's eyes were open.

"Hi, Gore!" Amy's blue eyes flooded with tears— tears of joy and relief at last.

"Hey there, buddy, thanks for waking up. You had us going there for a bit," I said.

He was dazed, but he appeared to be as good as he could be considering everything that had happened. His movements were purposeful, and he was moving his arms and legs separately, not like his previous posturing movements where both arms would move at the same time. It was the best moment of our lives.

> You're blessed when you feel you've lost what is most dear to you. Only then can you be embraced by the One most dear to you.
>
> Matthew 5:4 (The Message)

Amy

"Radiology called," Corrie said as we hovered over Gore's bed. "They can get Gore in for an MRI immediately, which is crazy-rare on a Friday. Let's just say it doesn't normally happen."

My stomach dropped. "I know this is a good thing, but..." There came my control issues. "No, go ahead. We will be ready." Dave and I both wanted to just sit and enjoy this victory a bit longer; we felt relieved and were fearful of any negative news to come raining down.

"Move on and trust, Amy," I whispered to myself inaudibly. The pain of watching your child lie there in a hospital bed, not knowing if he was ever going to wake up—and what kind of condition he might be in—is too gut wrenching to put into words, but we knew God had brought us this far.

Corrie and Laura proceeded to switch him over to an MRI-compliant bed and pole that wouldn't be pulled in by the magnet.

"Do you wanna come with Gore to the MRI?" Corrie asked. Of course we accepted, eager to leave the room and unwilling to let Gore leave our sight.

We waited through the MRI anxiously. When it was complete, we judged from Corrie's upbeat attitude and the looks on the technician's face that nothing seemed too bad—or was it wishful thinking?

"When will we know the results?" I asked.

"It'll take some time. Use this opportunity to go eat dinner and leave the room for a bit," Corrie suggested. True, we hadn't left the room in ages. Still, I was hesitant to go. "Don't worry," said Corrie, seeing the emotion etched on my face. "We promise to let you know when we hear anything at all. It's going to take a while for him to come out of the sedation. Please, you need a break."

Right then, I looked out the glass front of our room, and there was my brother, Russ. As had been the pattern the past few days, seeing someone for the first time brought an onslaught of tears. He wanted to start driving from Montana the night of the accident, but I told my mom to have him wait. The next day my mom inquired again about Russ coming.

"He wants to be here," she said.

"It's just so sad. I hate to bring him into this. Will you just tell him to wait another day?" I asked my mom. Well, he got tired of waiting, which was fine by me. I was glad to see him. We filled him in on the most recent turn of events, and we all headed out of the hospital together.

Once on the street, we breathed in as deeply as we could, purging our lungs of the hospital disinfectant air. The sun warmed our skin for the first time in what felt like eons. As we all started our walk toward a small cluster of restaurants on the corner, my phone rang. We had only made it a block.

"Hello?"

"Amy, it's Laura. We just heard back from the radiologist." I went rigid and gestured for Dave to come closer.

"M-R-I!" I mouthed.

"What's going on? What do they say?"

"The results are that there were no abnormalities!" announced Laura.

Did my ears deceive me?

"Nobody can believe it! They even had a second radiologist look at it to confirm the results." Laura spoke in a high-pitched voice. She certainly wasn't disguising her excitement.

"No abnormalities!" I exclaimed to my entire family. "We're coming back," I blurted out to Laura.

"No, you're not. Gore is going to need a while to come out of being sedated. Go eat. He won't be alone for a second."

"Thank you, Laura! Thank you so much!"

I clicked the phone off and screamed. Dave was doing the same, and in an instant, both of our faces streamed with the most joyous tears.

Did He ever show His glory! God did it. He gave us an MRI that showed nothing abnormal in our son that had been given a *less than one-percent chance* of having *any* brain function.

We all began to celebrate, hug, cry, and attempt to absorb the moment. What had just happened? Our family was given the greatest gift. We sat out on the patio of the restaurant calling every person that we could to pass along the wonderful news, knowing people were praying everywhere and waiting for the update. Doug had just left for the airport, so Dave was able to catch him and deliver the great news before his plane took off for Seattle.

However, it didn't take long for my thoughts to float elsewhere.

I kept thinking how we felt mere hours before, every time we walked down the hallway. The minute that we'd walk out of the room, the overwhelming, gut-wrenching reality settled in. Then the tears would pour down. As we passed other rooms, you could see the same painful look of despair in the eyes of the families around their loved one.

Often, as I'd exit the door to the PICU, I found a friend sitting in the waiting room that I didn't know was there. The difficulty of seeing someone and trying to piece together the ugly words of what happened resulted in sobbing. Usually I couldn't even speak; it was more than I could bear to say the words aloud. And what would I have said?

"Gore drowned."

"Gore nearly drowned."

"Gore died, and now he has a heartbeat and is being kept alive by machines, and we don't really think he is going to live."

It was literally unspeakable.

I knew Dave was thinking the same thing as he spoke at dinner of the pain we had seen the last few days. "Here we are, celebrating, yet there are those around us still broken, devastated, and unsure that they will ever leave with their child. I just want to be considerate of those people and get all our celebrating out now." It was quite a mood shift from the frenzy of excitement and utmost ecstasy, but it was so true. We were able to rejoice outside a few blocks from the hospital before we returned.

When we came back from dinner, Lukas was standing by our room grinning from ear to ear. No words needed to be spoken. We all hugged, cried, and thanked God for the grace He showed our family.

In learning more about the nature of Gore's accident and the type of injury that he had incurred, we discovered drowning victims have diffuse brain injuries. This means that not just one part of the brain is affected; it's all over. Sometimes if someone is in an accident where they hit their head, it will affect that one part of the brain. In drowning cases though, the injury usually runs throughout the brain. More often than not, the results are devastating. The MRI will show that the brain is just mush. Gore was underwater for over twenty minutes and without a heartbeat for at least fifty minutes. His brain was *not* mush. In fact, there were *no* abnormalities present. His blood was acidotic, his intestines were sloughing off from the cell death he experienced, yet his MRI appeared to be normal.

How is God's hand *not* in this? It's more of a struggle to explain away the miracle than to simply accept it's there, blaringly, obviously God's work. At that point, we had to wonder if He'd also bless our son with normal motor skills, overall functionality, and, perhaps most importantly, his personality...

Do you see it now? Do you see that I'm the one? Do you see that there's no god beside me? I bring death and I give life, I wound and I heal—there is no getting away from or around me!

Deuteronomy 32:39 (The Message)

ESKIMO KISSES:
SATURDAY

AMY

Saturday was momentous in a lot of ways, but it was also a big learning curve for us. Gore was awake and moving his arms and legs (a lot!) as if he were still trying to figure it all out. He was groggy from all the meds but also restless. His oxygen level was good, and he was basically breathing on his own—enough that they discussed taking him off his ventilator. That would be ideal because the more alert he became, the more he wanted it out. The nurses even had to restrain his hands just to keep him from grabbing it. Everyone was so shocked that he could be ready, but they agreed we should work toward it.

That day, Dave and I were graced with Katherine's presence. Katherine was my friend and fellow pledge sister from Baylor. Back then, she tried to help me through pre-med chemistry and biology—let's just say that today she is a doctor; I am not. I couldn't believe the text I received saying she was on the ground in Denver and headed to the hospital, just needing to know the room number. There were only a handful of people that could've walked into that situation and known how to handle it so well, and I knew she was one of them. Over the years, Dave and I have traveled with Katherine and her husband; just knowing Katherine, Dave felt relief for the support.

"This is great," I said to Dave. "She doesn't panic and can help us as another set of ears. She'll understand the medical terms and can translate."

Dave nodded emphatically. "I think because we're so tired and our brains are in information overload, we keep hearing two different interpretations from the doctors' explanations."

It was true. We were filtering what we wanted to hear from their information, a natural parental instinct. So much was happening that day, but Katherine was there to help us navigate through the explanation from the respiratory therapist. They wanted to hear a "leak" in preparation to remove the tube that had been aiding Gore. They had to be sure that once it was removed, his airway would remain open. I was ready for that tube to come out, because not only was it a sign of a brighter future, but it also meant we could hold him.

Here's another moment of truth. I inhaled deeply. Without incident, the tube was removed, and Gore's oxygen levels stayed up. They put a little oxygen mask next to him in case he needed it, but that was it.

Gore never had any major problems breathing. Little by little, all the tubes and lines came out; one by one, we began to eliminate issues. A neck brace had been placed on Gore due to concern that he could have easily hit his head while being carried underwater. The ditch is lined with rocks and large roots; yet remarkably, he seemed to have escaped injury during his long trip downstream. After his MRI on Friday, they made the decision that it could be removed. As soon as they took off the collar, they found a large pressure ulcer, which left a good size scar on his chin.

In between their apologies, we assured them, "In light of what could've been, this pales in comparison. If he walks out of here with a battle scar on his chin, we're going to be just fine with that."

"I have to hold him," I told Dave, eyes never deviating from Gore. This long-awaited, formerly improbable moment was finally here. For what seemed like forever, I had focused on his eyelashes. They were long, and because of his swelling, it was one of the few things that still looked like him. I'd stare at them to distract myself from the sterility of all the vents, tubes, and wires. Bending down over the blond, tan, scraped up little boy, I scooped him into my arms. He was heavy and groggy, but he was alive and moving, and his cheeks were pink again. It was a miraculous time. This kid, who I was *so* certain was dead, would restlessly crawl around in our arms. Previously, when he was in the bed covered with tubes, I would examine if there were any possible way that I could climb up there and lie next to him. I really couldn't see how I could make it work. Corrie had read my thoughts and said, "I know what you're thinking, and don't even think about it."

Although Gore didn't say much prior to the accident, we had taught him sign language to communicate with us—that is, if Ryan wasn't interpreting his every need and communicating them to us. These were basic signs like *eat*, *please*, *more*, *milk*, and everyday words. However, Gore didn't need to use many words since Ryan was always at his side insisting, "I know what he wants! He wants a glass of milk!" She'd say this while stooped down and protectively wrapping her arm around his little shoulders, stealing a kiss.

When Gore first arrived at Children's, a tube had been placed in his nose that traveled to his stomach for feeding during this whole ordeal. Today, the goal was to see if Gore could eat anything by himself.

"How about using the signs? It's worth a shot," Dave said.

I lowered my body to Gore's on the bed and said, "Hey, Gore! Do you want to eat?" I enunciated each word slowly and also formed the sign for *eat*. One more time for good measure. Holding my breath, I waited hopefully for a sign of comprehension.

He quickly moved his little fist to his mouth and gave the sign for "eat" right back!

We crowded around him, seeing what he did or didn't know. Each time we got a response, all of us praised him as if it were his first accomplishment.

"Say 'please'!" I communicated the sign simultaneously.

Sure enough, Gore rubbed his hand in a small circle on his chest as he had always done for "please."

This kid must've been hungry; he's working for food, I thought facetiously through tears. These were the first indications that Gore remembered what he knew before. Dave, wiping away tears, walked up to him and tried something that he taught Gore before the accident. We were on a roll. Why stop?

"Gore, can you give Daddy Eskimo kisses?"

Gore never understood that he was supposed to put his nose against Dave's, but he would instantly start shaking his head back and forth as if he were rubbing Dave's nose with his.

Gore sleepily looked at Dave and started shaking his head back and forth. We couldn't believe it! He was coming back, and we soaked in every second of it. My mom texted our family, "He just did Eskimo kisses!" All summer, everyone laughed each time Gore was instructed to give Eskimo kisses, as he immediately shook his head. We all understood the significance of the moment.

Shortly after this, he started drinking from a bottle and then eating a banana. The nurses seemed quite surprised. We still weren't grasping how all-encompassing a diffuse brain injury should be, so they explained that often kids with this kind of injury had to relearn to swallow, suck, or cough. At the time, this didn't appear to be an issue for Gore. All the unimaginable things we had prayed for were taking place.

> There's more to come: We continue to shout our praise even when we're hemmed in with troubles, because we know how troubles can develop passionate patience in us, and how

that patience in turn forges the tempered steel of virtue, keeping us alert for whatever God will do next. In alert expectancy such as this, we're never left feeling shortchanged. Quite the contrary—we can't round up enough containers to hold everything God generously pours into our lives through the Holy Spirit!

Romans 5:3-5 (The Message)

The Worst of Days

Dave

I bet we'll be out by Tuesday.

I hesitate to even admit that thought crossed my mind. Gore was doing so well, or so we thought.

With Amy's mom, sister, and Katherine still there, I had taken a break from the hospital to go to my office and clean up a few lingering things. Not ready to face anyone from work yet, I thought that Sunday would give me the only opportunity to sneak in and out without having to talk to anyone. It was still impossible for me to talk with any unknowing person without breaking down.

Returning to the hospital that afternoon, I saw that Gore was moved to the eighth floor, no longer enjoying the luxury of one-on-one care in the PICU. *Must be the good progress*, I thought. But a surprise greeted me.

Gore's eyes were rolling around in his head as if nothing was connecting. He couldn't track objects or people. He couldn't do sign language as he had the day before, nor could he Eskimo kiss.

Locking my eyes on Amy's across the room, I shot an alarmed look. "What's going on?"

"It may take three to four days for him to fully metabolize the drugs," said a nurse. This appeared more serious than just a drug-related issue. He had been pretty irritable; he wasn't crying, but he looked uncomfortable and fussy.

"Is he in pain? Could this be a reaction to the drugs? He seems so agitated," I said, unwittingly crossing my arms to comfort myself.

Everyone mentioned similar possibilities: it could be the drugs, but irritability is completely normal for a brain injury like Gore's.

"You can expect it," doctors would say. "We can give him Tylenol in case he's feeling pain from the tube, which might've made his throat sore, or his chest from the compressions." But it sounded as if they were grasping for answers themselves.

We hated imagining Gore in pain, but concern for his eyesight, hearing, and other brain-related abnormalities were at the forefront of my mind.

He seemed so normal on Saturday—okay, not normal, but considering everything, he seemed much better than this. Was the MRI ordered too early after he was warmed up? Could there be brain damage that wasn't picked up by the MRI? Disconcerting to me was that Gore's mobility weakened. He pinned his arms to his side, moving them less and less. His eyes remained half open while sleeping, which looked eerie.

"I'm ordering a neurological consult for Monday," said the doctor on call.

No doubt, Amy and I appeared discouraged.

"I just don't know how to feel right now," I said. We just came off the miracle of an MRI showing no abnormalities, but then suddenly, our son "wasn't there." He would look right through us like he was in an alternate dimension. Indeed, he was an unmoving, silent apparition. My stomach churned just watching him.

"Since I left earlier today, the change has been so dramatic, and as much as I want to believe it's just the drugs wearing off, it doesn't make sense that he would be much more alert and 'there' and then be *this* spacey and immobile," I worried.

Meanwhile, Mary Lynn had just arrived from Gunnison, and Katherine was flying back to Texas. Before Katherine left, she reminded Amy and me how miraculous this was. "As someone who has seen a lot as a doctor, I have never experienced anything like this. I know there's uncertainty, but right now he's alive against all odds."

After becoming accustomed to the one-on-one care of the PICU, we weren't getting that on our new floor. We wanted answers. Realizing that the hospital was quiet on a Sunday night, we accepted that we must wait until Monday morning.

> The Lord is my rock, my fortress, and my savior; my God is my rock, in whom I find protection. He is my shield, the power that saves me, and my place of safety.
>
> Psalm 18:2 (NLT)

MONDAY

AMY

First thing Monday morning on rounds, we were full of questions. We were introduced to Dr. Bernard, the attending neurologist. He could sense our anxiety, was instantly receptive, and reassured us that they would do whatever they could to cover all the options.

"It could be anything from seizures, which might be simple to correct with medication."

That is exactly what it seemed like to me (in my "extensive medical opinion"). Meanwhile, we glanced at Gore. He would look at everyone for one second and then "go dark." Right then it was as if he couldn't see us.

"We're going to get Endocrinology involved. They have a list of things that they want to check, from his thyroid to a type of diabetes. We'll get another EEG and MRI scheduled right away as well," he continued. "I also think that we need to check his eyes. I'm worried there might be some problems with his sight."

"Great, let's do it! We're completely on board. Get every person, department, and every possible test that you deem necessary to get some answers," Dave and I quickly agreed.

Prior to this, Dave repeated, "I think something is wrong with his eyes," dispersing a few "or maybe it is the drugs" phrases along with them. Both of us were living in a world where these were the *only* possible explanations. God was giving us a few more lessons in trust. To come off such a high on Friday and Saturday and then see him regressing so rapidly in front of our eyes were "some of the worst days," as Dave said later.

But, little by little, every test was coming back negative. Endocrinology couldn't find anything wrong. Neurology ordered another MRI for Tuesday and another EEG on Monday evening. As each result trickled in, we once again felt thankful for positive results but also confused from the lack of answers.

The EEG was especially eye opening, to say the least. The same lady who hooked Gore up to his first EEG once again attached all the electrodes to Gore's head and prepared the computer screen once more. We weren't sure what to expect since all we knew were flat lines. She turned it on, and I almost fell over.

"The lines are crazy-wavy!" I sputtered, realizing the contrast since the first day here. We truly had no idea what we were looking at. They were moving up and down and all over. After being hooked up for only about half an hour, the results came back with some "slowing," but there was no indication of seizures. They weren't concerned. Discovering that there were no seizures meant there wasn't a quick fix with medication, but I was ultimately glad that it was one less hurdle to overcome.

We were scared, but then God gave us that gift, that little piece of hope that we needed to get to the next day: that EEG, a thousand times better than the one in the PICU. Once again, I felt God saying, "Here I am, still in control."

> "For I know the plans I have for you," declares
> the LORD, "plans to prosper you and not to

harm you, plans to give you hope and a future. Then you will call upon me and come and pray to me, and I will listen to you. You will seek me and find me when you seek me with all your heart."

Jeremiah 29: 11-13 (NIV)

TUESDAY

AMY

Officially one week since the accident.

My dad and brother had gone over to Gunnison to help take care of Kirk and Ryan along with my brother-in-law and their kids. They were anxious to start building a better fence around that irrigation ditch. My mom, Anne, and Mary Lynn stayed since they could tell Gore's state was uncertain and back on the roller coaster.

After another MRI, the results for the brain were the same: no abnormalities. The spine, on the other hand, revealed a "signal" (abnormal area) that was present on the first MRI of the spine but was "so insignificant with the way Gore was presenting" that they didn't even address it.

"This cannot be operated on," explained Dr. Bernard, "nor is it in a problematic area. There's not even any swelling. However, it could be causing Gore's immobility." *Okay, two MRIs showing the same thing* (my selective hearing was in play). I was just relieved that maybe, *maybe* Gore's lovable personality would start to creep back. *One thing at a time,* I reminded myself. Whatever the answer, he was going to need some help.

We met with the team of rehabilitation doctors. They felt Gore needed long-term rehabilitation, so we'd move to the rehab floor as soon as they had space and authorization from our insurance. It would take a few days. We would live there for an unknown period of time that had been targeted at four to six weeks.

In the meantime, we were still able to begin Gore's therapy sessions. Initially I was upbeat. "The strides we've made in a week are incredible," Dave said. "A week ago, we didn't know if he'd wake up." I agreed. To think that Gore even had the potential to move again was inspiring.

These feelings quickly transitioned to pain.

The physical therapist gently lowered Gore to the ground. Gore's empty face stared ahead at a distant point before it landed in the carpet. There he lay, wiggling as if he were a newborn.

Tears streaming down my face, I turned away. It was hard to imagine him running around like the wild kid that he was just a week before, the kid who made me crazy most days with his sheer destruction, all the while melting my heart with his reaffirming hugs.

Dave looked at me with concern; Mary Lynn quietly watched.

"It's going to be okay. I don't want to cry, but I just don't know how long he'll be like this," I said, trying to hide my tears on Mary Lynn's shoulder.

"It doesn't matter if it takes ten years until he can walk again. It doesn't matter, but he *will* walk, Amy." Dave was positive, which I appreciated.

It's tough to wrestle with being thankful that your child is alive when the outcome *could* have been devastating. I stared at that same child, formerly extremely mobile, now literally like a newborn at square one.

Turning back toward Gore, new waves of pain jolted me. He wasn't crying *at all* anymore. There was absolutely no sound or expression from him. This staring, along with his blank, solemn expression, was almost harder to watch than his physical setbacks. Although, selfishly, walking was in the back of my mind, I just wanted to see Gore's personality return. I needed his smile, his laugh, that gleam in his eye…

"Why is he so robotic? No emotions, no indication that he knows us?" I asked, my stomach in knots. This wasn't the first time, nor would it be the last, that I asked this question.

The answer was always the same: "This is normal for someone with a brain injury."

But I thought there wasn't a brain injury! I screamed inside. *The MRI is normal!* My old "friend" Guilt knocked at my door again, trying to linger within my heart. Still, I was wrestling constantly with the thought that this should never have happened. It didn't have to. How had I let my guard down?

I wanted to believe that God had ordained July 6, 2010 and the days before and the days to come. I realized sitting and wallowing in guilt was *not* part of

God's bigger plan. My guilt and my feelings don't take precedence over that plan. It's bigger than anything I'd ever be able to understand; it trumps *everything*.

Dave's sister, Sherri, had arrived. We quickly had accepted her offer to fly out from Seattle. My mom, Anne, and Mary Lynn all left, and I felt I needed someone that was like a sister to be near. She always had the most calming demeanor, and the kids loved her. Her presence alone was reassuring. Sherri, being so intuitive, had already begun to pray for my guilt and Gore's smile.

> Therefore if anyone *is* in Christ, *he is* a new creation; the old *things* have passed away; behold, new *things* have come.
>
> 2 Corinthians 5:17 (LEB)

WEDNESDAY

AMY

> I wait for the Lord, my soul waits, and in His word, I put my hope.
>
> Psalm 130:5 (NIV)

I started keeping a journal that day and wrote this verse down as the mantra most befitting my current mind-set.

We knew Gore was improving every day, but we had to wait and learn patience. His progress seemed painfully slow, though we had no concept of how long progress takes (or if it occurs at all). We met the doctor in charge of Gore's care, Dr. Oleszek, and instantly felt good about our long-term commitment to living on the rehabilitation floor. Just as in the PICU, we had two therapists we were fortunate to work with. Gretchen was Gore's physical therapist (PT) and Amanda was his occupational therapist (OT) during the week. They were Gore's "personal trainers," as Dave joked. They worked with him twice a day "two-a-days." Similar to Corrie and Lukas, they were an encouraging pair who never ceased recognizing Gore's progress.

"He's doing so great! He's making promising improvement!" they would say enthusiastically.

Sunday, Monday, and Tuesday were some of the toughest days. His rapid regression made it seem as if Gore would never be normal again. Then, just about the time we had exhausted every option and the response "we can't find anything wrong" prevailed, he would make progress. In spite of my initial shock, once Gore got going, his daily improvement was subtle, yet significant. Even from the morning therapy sessions to the afternoon sessions, there were dramatic changes. By Tuesday, his eyes began to track better, and his motion in his arms improved. Each day his progress was just enough to encourage us to the next.

Walking back from PT/OT, I saw Lily's familiar eyes fixed on us. It seemed like so long ago that I had seen those eyes while we were in such a fog. I caught myself staring at her.

"I'm Lily. I was the nurse who took Gore off the helicopter that first night and was with him in the PICU," she began.

"Oh, we remember who you are. We're just surprised to see you," I said.

"I had to come and see Gore with my own eyes."

"Of course. Where have you been? We've missed you."

Lily spoke to us, but her eyes moved toward Gore. "I was off for a few days so I assumed the worst when I came back and he was no longer in the PICU. I couldn't believe it when everyone told me that he had been moved to another floor." She shook her head and smiled at us, eyes brimming with emotion. "It's amazing. He's here and improving. This is one of the most pleasant surprises I've ever seen."

I glanced at Dave, who looked as appreciative as I felt.

Gore's case was wondrous. I don't think I fully grasped it at the time, but I was counting my blessings.

> He performs *wonders* that cannot be fathomed,
> miracles that cannot be counted.

Job 5:9 (NIV)

THURSDAY

DAVE

Amy and I woke up, and Gore was sleeping soundly as ever—but with his arms spread out above his head!

141

"Look, Dave!" Amy whispered while turning my face toward Gore. I thought surely she'd swoop on Gore, wake him up, and shower him with affection. He was barely able to use his arms the past four days; they were pinned at his side constantly. To know that he could even get them both above his head was huge progress! I reminded myself not to wake Gore up in my enthusiasm.

Likewise, in his morning PT/OT session, he couldn't hold his head up on his own. By that afternoon, he was holding it up without any help for long stretches of time. We could not believe our eyes! In a matter of hours, he made extraordinary strides that we once worried would take weeks, months, or more.

In simple terms, Gore slept a lot, which is normal with his type of injury but also necessary because he needed sleep for all those little wires in his brain to reconnect. That lack of expression and emotion, so troubling to us, slowly gave way to signs of the old Gore coming back. When he first started to make sounds again, it sounded like a cat's meow. We sat and laughed as we heard him making these strange sounds, but it was music to our ears.

Thursday, Coach and Jody came to visit—the first time Coach had seen Gore since that terrible first night sitting in the hallway of the PICU.

"Gore!" he shouted in an attempt to be upbeat. His eyes revealed his true feelings, though; they glistened immediately. I couldn't help but think about his tears that night sitting outside Gore's room. Scooping Gore up, he refused to set him down the rest of the afternoon.

Paperwork was done, and a room was now available for us on the rehab floor. We were feeling confident this was a positive move and more conducive to Gore's multiple therapy sessions. Per hospital tradition, a nurse walked in with a red wagon to pull Gore away to his new room.

"No, it's okay. I'd like to carry him if you're okay with that," said Coach to the nurse. It was touching to see him cradling Gore's tiny body closely to him, unlike the last time he held Gore in his arms.

Even though Gore was barely holding his head up on his own, this was a much better day, and Coach wasn't giving him up. He held him for hours, clutching him while we relocated to a new floor. Even with his jaw set bravely, the tears in his eyes appeared frequently.

Coach told us that every day back in Gunnison, he walked to the irrigation ditch to attempt to make sense of it all. He explained that in spite of what happened there, he would sit right where they laid Gore. "It's encouraging and therapeutic. Strangely, I always leave feeling better," he said. "It's like God whispers to me that he's still at work. I pray and I feel His presence."

He explained what happened the first morning he returned to Gunnison after Gore's accident. He sat in the brush on the bank near where Gore was found. Sunlight glittered on the ditch's rushing waters as a spotlight on the unforgettable scene. Glancing down, he noticed two sticks. One stick lay horizontally across another stick *forming a cross*. Coach scrambled up, ran to the barn, grabbed some wire, and came right back. Quickly wiring the sticks together, he then placed the cross on the bank right where Gore had been given CPR. The horizontal stick has one little section at the end that sticks up, and on the other end, there's a part that points down, "like two little hands," he said. It's still there, on the bank, in the exact spot where we thought Gore had been taken from us.

> Instead of worrying, pray. Let petitions and praises shape your worries into prayers, letting God know your concerns. Before you know it, a sense of God's wholeness, everything coming together for good, will come and settle you down. It's wonderful what happens when Christ displaces worry at the center of your life.
>
> Philippians 4:6-7 (The Message)

Amy

Gore hadn't slept in a crib at home for quite some time. Although he wasn't yet two years old, he refused to be confined to one. We didn't put it past him to climb on the rails and jump off. That thought alone kept me from sleeping at night, so we gave him a twin-sized bed early on.

When Gore was first moved to the rehabilitation floor, he wasn't moving. The decision was made to put him in a crib, which felt wrong in so many ways. It was as if he reverted to infancy. The small crib was just a reminder that he wasn't even rolling over, much less jumping out.

As Gore's movements progressed, they also became spastic. For safety reasons, we all agreed to put him in a Posey bed, a twin size hospital bed with a tent-like structure over it. You had to unzip it to climb in, but it was soft if Gore were to fall against it, unlike the previous metal crib. I'd crawl in with him in the evenings as he dozed off and in the mornings as he awoke, so it proved therapeutic for me as well.

One night, Gore rolled to the edge of the bed and would've fallen off but for the tent holding him in. He lay very still between the side of the bed and tent, his face pressed up against the mesh. I quickly jumped up and pushed him back onto the bed, thinking that he was stuck and wouldn't like that. Almost as soon as I sat down, he rolled right back in the extra fabric on the edge of the bed and was still once more.

He's not laughing or crying. What do I think? Once more, I moved to help him out. This time I saw beginnings of a smirk and the mischievous look in his eyes.

"You're doing this on purpose!" I cried. I was only playfully indignant. Gore's eye gleamed as it had before, when he was doing something that he wasn't supposed to. He couldn't laugh yet, but I saw the corners of his mouth curl up as if the laughter wanted to escape. After moving him back onto the bed, I told Dave what I thought was happening. Sure enough, Gore rolled right back in the gap, his crooked smirk returning.

"Dave, he's coming back!" I said triumphantly, wanting to laugh and cry and celebrate at this achievement. It was the first sign that his good-natured personality would return. That's what I missed more than *anything*.

Not only was Gore's personality returning, but our other kids returned to us as well. One of the worst thoughts I had in the PICU was trying to explain to Ryan and Kirk what happened to Gore. Ryan held a special place in her heart for him and adored, loved, and cared for him so well. We had constantly reminded her to take her hands and lips off him, but she truly couldn't help herself. "Goresky" was her real, live baby doll. While Kirk was younger than Ryan and wouldn't understand the magnitude of what had happened, Ryan undoubtedly would.

"I know the hospital isn't the ideal place for children and they're in perfect hands with my family in Gunnison, but I'm at my breaking point," I told Dave, holding a picture of all three kids in my hands.

"I agree," said Dave. "It's been thirteen days. They need their parents."

Wow, thirteen days. By far the longest bout of separation from Kirk and Ryan we've ever experienced.

"There is the walking question…" Dave reminded me of our conundrum. We had met with the Family Services coordinator to discuss which messages we should communicate to Kirk and Ryan, what was appropriate and what was *too* much information. Gore only just started to hold his head up on his own and could sit with the aid of the Bumbo seat, a booster seat that had a structure in the front to hold his torso upright. Unsure of what their response would be at learning he was unable to walk, I was apprehensive.

"Still better than the alternative." I referenced my darkest fears in the PICU. We decided we'd just have to play it by ear.

Pacing the room feeling anxious yet excited about Kirk and Ryan's arrival with my parents, I'd stare out the window, analyze all the equipment in the room to think through the questions they might ask, and then walk over to Gore to love on him.

Soon, Ryan and Kirk's high, energetic voices floated down the hallway to our ears.

"I'm gonna squeeze him so hard!" Ryan said, her voice bouncing from what was certainly skipping.

Their volume increased, and Dave and I stood by each other with fluttering nerves and big smiles. Suddenly, they burst in. Ryan was dressed up with her play-jewelry, and the usually relaxed Kirk wore an unparalleled grin.

"Goresky!" Ryan yelled, preparing to race over to him.

Dave and I turned our eyes toward Gore, unsure of his reaction. To our amazement, Gore's face lit up. His recognition of his siblings was unmistakable. We had been able to get occasional small laughs out of him with persistent tickling and smiles—always with coaxing. Not this time. He saw them and smiled from ear to ear. It was as if the light turned on, and he said, "There they are. Those are my people! Where have you been?" Gore's jubilant, rosy cheeks were soon smothered with Ryan's kisses and Kirk's devoted attention.

It was a moment that will forever be one of our greatest memories. I experienced healing in those few minutes that I hadn't experienced in two weeks. You could see the light in Gore's eyes again; our kids needed each other. We were all together, and the world seemed right. We *were* going to get through this.

❖

The days were running together. We fell into our daily routine of PT/OT and speech therapy until the day we had been waiting for. It was July 25, 2010.

Dave's mom, Marcia, had flown in from Seattle to help us with the kids. That particular day, Dave had run home to be with them, which left Gore and me in the hospital that morning. After I crawled into his tent bed with him, he started saying his favorite word over and over: "*Nnnnoooo.*" It started out slowly, and after each outburst, I would repeat him. The more he said it, the louder and more emphatic he became.

"*No!*"

As I laughed uncontrollably, Gore's face cracked in a grin as he began to chuckle too. *This is good enough for me for the rest of the week*, I thought joyously.

But it gets even better.

We went to PT/OT about 11:45 a.m. Laura was waiting for us and announced, "Today, we're going to have Gore crawl." Uh oh. *This isn't going to be good.* He became cranky when placed on his hands and knees, as he hadn't crawled in therapy yet. Holding my breath, I watched Laura stoop down to position Gore on the floor. Immediately, I saw Gore trucking around on the ground as if he'd been crawling before without issue.

"Wow! Go, Gore!" I was thrilled and cheering him on, delighted at the sight.

"Since he's doing so well, let's graduate him to walking with a cart," said Laura. Fastening his little hands on it, she led Gore to walk around. Simply putting weight on his legs and standing upright was an incredible accomplishment. His progress this day was remarkable. He decided he didn't want the cart, so she grabbed his hands and led him around the room. He was doing great for a short distance, and then he stopped, dropped his hands, and stood for a moment like he was thinking.

"Look how good he's standing!"

"His balance has improved so much."

"Good job, Gore!"

As we flooded his ears with praise, Gore took a step. Then another.

He was *walking* without any help.

After seven steps on his own, he stopped. Of course I started to cry, remembering his first day of therapy. There he was, learning to hold himself up as if he were a newborn incapable of any independent tasks. I cried tears of pain then. This time there was only a continuous stream of euphoric, thankful tears. Best of all, Gore did it all with that big grin on his face. He was not only functioning but also performing tasks with his personality shining through. I couldn't believe it, but I will never forget it. Really, the whole process was remarkable.

Afterward, Gore conked out. He absolutely deserved that nap and knew it.

> In that day he will remove the cloud of gloom,
> the shadow of death that hangs over the earth.
> He will swallow up death forever! The Sovereign
> Lord will wipe away all tears.
>
> Isaiah 25:7-8 (NLT)

THE RELEASE

W^e couldn't contain him anymore. All the nurses on the floor knew it. His PT, Gretchen, knew it. His OT, Amanda, knew it. He was done. He was bored hanging around the hospital, and it was time to go home. Now that he was walking, he ventured out to the nurses' station every chance he had to say hello. He had figured out how to unzip his Posey bed, so that wasn't keeping him contained anymore.

It was time. As we discussed Gore's release, we were tearful saying our good-byes to our very faithful doctors and therapists. Dr. Oleszek recalled our first days in rehab. "My heart sank when I read Gore's chart before seeing him for the first time. Then, after meeting him, even though he couldn't hold up his head or roll over, his eyes focused on mine, and I thought, 'He's in there.'"

She described his daily, often hourly functional gains over the last three weeks as exceeding her expectations and his incredible recovery as an inspiration. "My philosophy on the rehabilitation unit is 'never say never,' and Gore exemplifies that."

She gave us the "go ahead," and we started packing.

On August 2nd, we walked out of the hospital pulling our red wagons full of our belongings. We needed a wagon for all of Gore's stuffed animals alone—priceless. We said good-bye to the nurses and then stopped by the coffee shop to thank everyone we grew to know so well. Gore was able to give his small wave now and say, "Bye-bye!" It was surreal watching everyone's smiling, sometimes tear-streaked faces bid us farewell while Gore, healthy and rosy cheeked once more, waved to everybody like they were his best friends.

As we left, we passed by the elevators that first carried us up to the PICU twenty-seven days before. I shuddered as I thought about that night and those first few days. Each time I entered those elevators, the tears flowed. I prayed for every family in there, "God, give them strength. Heal their children. Give them hope in their brokenness. Extend Your grace and mercy to them."

Even in our victory, we would never forget those still suffering. After all, we were there once, with a "less than one percent" chance.

We drove home that day. Gore toddled inside and, within a few minutes, began to hide his toys in the floor vents, just like before, as if he'd never left.

> For it is with your heart that you believe and are justified, and it is with your mouth that you profess your faith and are saved. As the Scripture says, "Anyone who believes in him will never be put to shame."
>
> Romans 10:10-11 (NIV)

The Reflections

The "What Ifs?"

Each day we learned something new about what took place the night of July 6. Sometimes I can't process what I know to be true "medical" facts and what I see in front of my eyes. Here is this little boy, grinning from ear to ear, who shouldn't be here according to practically everyone. It's hard to even hear some of the information, even though I know there was a purpose.

I often felt that familiar nagging thought of "what if"…what if Coach hadn't found him when he did? What if my dad, Suzanne, and Don hadn't been there to give him CPR? What if the paramedics had given up once they got there and heard how long he had been under water? What if they hadn't called CareFlight? What if they hadn't decided to "cool" him? What if hundreds if not thousands of people hadn't prayed? What if God didn't answer our prayers the way we wanted?

There are many questions that we talk about often, but the one that keeps me awake at night is, What if the outcome were different? Could we still see the purpose and know that God is faithful? I pray with all my heart that we could. It's a hard thought with which I wrestle.

When each "What if?" creeps into my mind, I remind myself that each precarious situation that could've turned out so differently, so *easily*, is evidence of master design. Everything aligned ideally to produce the outcome we received. From the doctors' and paramedics' resolve to our family's involvement, God's hand guided in the situation. God's plans stretch the ages.

> God possesses infinite knowledge and an awareness that is uniquely His. At all times, even in the midst of any type of suffering, I can realize that He knows, loves, watches, understands, and more than that, He has a purpose.
>
> Billy Graham

God and Medicine

Not everybody's story will end like this. There seems to be no rhyme or reason for why the results are the way they are. Today, clinical studies are ongoing regarding hypothermic treatment and the effects for children Gore's age. We hope that they continue these studies and exploring all the medical options for drowning and cardiac arrest situations. In Gore's case, the general consensus is along the lines of, "We just don't know why he had the outcome he did. We don't know if it had anything to do with the hypothermic treatment or not. This is inexplicable." Gore's story is a medical mystery.

Let's take a look at the following predictors of poor outcome paired with Gore's presentation.

Prediction of poor outcome if:

1. Duration of submersion time to effective CPR is greater than 10 minutes (Gore was under water for more than 20 minutes.)

2. Duration of resuscitation is greater than 25 minutes. (Gore's was almost 30 minutes.)

3. Age is less than three years. (Gore was 22 months.)

4. Glasgow Coma Score, or GCS*, is less than 5. (Gore's was 3 in Gunnison and 4 in Denver.)

5. Requirement of continued CPR in the ED. (Gore required CPR for an extended period of time in Gunnison and was still receiving Epinephrine and Atropine after arrival in the Denver ED.)

6. pH is less than 7.1 more than three hours after the incident. (Gore's was 6.89.)

   Additionally, studies show a 100 percent mortality rate (rate of long-term negative consequences) when the time to initial CPR is greater than twenty minutes.

   (Source: Fuhrman & Zimmerman – Pediatric Critical Care Fourth Edition)

*GCS is a neurological scale that aims to give a reliable, objective way of recording the conscious state of a person. A patient is assessed against the criteria of the scale. The resulting points give a patient the lowest possible score of 3 (indicating deep unconsciousness) up to a 15.

DATE: 7/6/10   G. Otteson   PT. IDENTIFICATION ____

GUNNISON VALLEY HOSPITAL EMERGENCY DEPT.
TRAUMA PROGRESS

```
248619   RM-            345613      P/T-ER
OTTESON GORE D          F    1
SHERMAN RO      07/06/10  B/D 09/22/08
```

MECHANISM OF INJURY: drowning _____

TREATMENT/MEDS/VS IN FIELD: CPR, IO, epi x 1, Monitor _____

CHIEF COMPLAINT: asystole, CPR, apneic _____

UPON ARRIVAL: (CHECK APPROPRIATELY) ✓
✓ IV (IF YES, SITE: IO Rt leg ✓ OXYGEN BVM ✓ MONITOR
✓ SPINAL
____ INTUBATED (____ nasal or ____ oral) ____ OTHER _____

TRAUMA SCORE

REVISED TRAUMA SCORE

Area of Measurement	Coded Value
Systolic Blood Pressure (mmHG)	
>89	4
76-89	3
50-75	2
1-49	1
0	⓪
Respiratory Rate (spontaneous inspirations/minute)*	
10-29	4
>29	3
6-9	2
1-5	1
0	⓪
*patient initiated, not artificial ventilations	
Glasgow Coma Scale Score	
13-15	4
9-12	3
6-8	1
4-5	1
3	⓪
Total Possible Points	0-12

GLASGOW COMA SCORE

GLASGOW COMA SCORE

Areas of Response	Points
Eye Opening	
Eyes open spontaneously	4
Eyes open in response to voice	3
Eyes open in response to pain	②
No eye opening response	1
Best Verbal Response	
Oriented, e.g., to person, place, time	5
Confused, speaks but is disoriented	4
Inappropriate, but comprehensible words	3
Incomprehensible sounds but no words are spoken	2
None	①
Best Motor Response	
Obeys command to move	6
Localized painful stimulus	5
Withdraws from painful stimulus	4
Flexion, abnormal decorticate posturing	3
Extension, abnormal decerebrate posturing	②
No movement or posturing	1
Total Possible Points	3-15
Major Head Injury	≥8
Moderate Head Injury	9-12
Minor Head Injury	13-15

TRAUMA SCORE: 0
TIME: 1940
INITIALS: SL

GLASGOW SCORE: 3
TIME: 1940
INITIALS: SL

———◆———

When we took Gore to visit the hospital in Gunnison, Dr. Sherman and others involved with Gore's care referred to him as "the miracle boy." Tisha, the respiratory therapist, told us, "He's a child, and that's what drove us to keep going in spite of how hopeless it was." She went on to explain, "The saying goes 'you have to be warm and dead to be pronounced dead.' Gore was freezing cold."

They described an ethical dilemma which came into play for many of the medical staff. The concern was, "Why drag this poor family through such an ordeal? We're just prolonging the inevitable." Because, for every result like Gore's, there are at least a million other cases that don't turn out favorably. Tisha remembers being "so happy yet so sad" about securing a heartbeat. Dr. Sherman and Barb, the RN on duty, looked at each other after they put Gore on the helicopter and questioned, "Did we do the right thing?" or had they saved a child who would ultimately have no brain activity?

Those that were in Gunnison, along with medical records, contribute to this timeline from that night, as well as important medical explanations:

- 6:45 – Gore was last seen in the cabin. The search began.

- 7:09 – Gore was found 325 feet downstream submerged approximately 18 inches below water pinned against a log.

- Nancy called 911.

- CPR began immediately and continued until paramedics took over.

- 7:14 – The ambulance arrived.

- 7:25 – Gore arrived at Gunnison Valley Hospital. He did not have a pulse.

- Gore's temperature had dropped to eighty-three degrees Fahrenheit.

- Because Gore was "cold and dead" and not "warm and dead," they were in it—a debate not uncommon in the medical world. *How much* does a doctor intervene? *When* is it prudent to quit? How do you tell the family that it's time to quit? No one wants to stop, but knowing what all the statistics and odds say, you don't want to prolong the inevitable or draw out a family's pain.

- Gunnison hospital continued trying to resuscitate him and administered several rounds of epinephrine and atropine in an effort to jump-start Gore's heart.

- 7:41 – Gore demonstrated a palpable pulse.

- His pupils were fixed and dilated; this suggests massive brain injury.

- 8:45 – Gore left Gunnison on CareFlight.

- According to the paramedic on CareFlight, the amount of electricity they put through his body to keep his heart beating (the medical term is *pacing*) was more than most adults require.

- 10:12 p.m. – Gore arrived in Denver.

- Acidotic blood is the result of hypoxia (insufficient oxygen). This was occurring with Gore. Our bodies have a perfect pH of 7.35. When a body is deprived of oxygen for a long period of time, cell death occurs, and acid is released. The more acid, the lower the number on the scale. Anything under 7 is very concerning. As stated, when Gore was checked the first time in Denver, his pH was 6.89.

- You cannot pronounce someone brain dead when they are not at normal body temperature. Gore was still cold from the water in the irrigation ditch. Everyone seemed to agree that they would send him to the PICU to "warm up" to his normal temperature and then perform a battery of tests to assess his brain functionality.

- Gore's CT looked normal, but they told us that was not surprising because swelling on the brain usually occurred in the first 48 to 72 hours and probably wouldn't show up this early.

- For hypothermic treatment to occur successfully, the PICU's protocol was initiation within six hours. Gore was just outside of the six-hour mark, starting closer to seven hours out.

- 2:00 a.m. – Hypothermic Treatment and the waiting began.

After discussions with doctors, such as Dr. Carpenter at Children's Hospital Colorado and Dr. Sherman from Gunnison Valley Hospital, Gore's story is examined from a variety of angles.

Dr. Sherman says this is why Gore's case is "most interesting and compelling." Even though he's "not religious," he says, "This is a miracle, and I believe the possibility that Mammalian Diving Reflex (MDR) played a role in Gore's amazing outcome."

Dr. Sherman goes on to explain that MDR is a sort of hibernation that allows a mammal to stay under water for an extended period of time without damage to the brain. The diving reflex is triggered by cold water contacting the face. He believes Gore's submersion in cold water for twenty-five minutes caused Gore's body to respond in this manner. "While the water wasn't icy, it was still cold, and there's just no other explanation."

On the other hand, Dr. Carpenter, the attending physician in the PICU at Children's, is skeptical of the MDR theory for several reasons. First, as mentioned, the water temperature, although cold in a mountain river or ditch in the summer, was not ice cold and therefore not likely protective. Also, the MDR is not consistently present in humans. It requires the heart to continue beating to provide protection, whereas Gore's heart had stopped before he was found.

When asked his opinion of what led to Gore's recovery, Dr. Carpenter described a mentor that he had back in medical school who always said, "There are two types of people in medicine: believers and non-believers," referring to belief in the power of medical science. He goes on to say:

> Ultimately, "believers" feel that their knowledge, skill, and medical decision-making are largely responsible for their patients' outcomes. On the other hand, "non-believers" are doctors who more explicitly recognize that there are significant limitations to what medicine can do and what they as people can do to influence the end result for their patients. They leave room for the unexplained phenomena—good or bad.

Dr. Carpenter sits in the latter camp. Although not religious either, he has witnessed both good and bad outcomes that he cannot fully explain, Gore included.

There are certainly different perspectives about Gore's condition and how his outcome is possible. There's Mammalian Diving Reflex, medical phenomena, and divine intervention. While most professionals in the medical world agree that colder water is always better than warm, the temperature at which the water provides a protective component for the brain is unclear. We know that the water in the ditch that time of year was precisely 55 degrees because fly fishermen in that camp take the temperature regularly for fishing purposes.

Regardless of your religious views, medical professionals are perplexed, tossing around the terms "miracle" and "higher powers at work." There is still the fact that there was *less than one-percent* chance of Gore ever resuming normal brain function and making a complete recovery. It doesn't make sense, but we're not complaining. We know that it took a team of deft and dedicated doctors and nurses to produce this outcome, but we also know that God performed a miracle. Medicine and God don't have to conflict in an either/or dichotomy; they work in conjunction with one another. There is only so much humans and medicine can achieve, so at our limits, we believe God intervened to fully heal Gore's brain. He performs miracles every day, and this is just one example of His power and might on this side of heaven.

> But I have raised you up for this very purpose,
> that I might show you my *power and* that my
> name might be proclaimed in all the earth.
>
> Exodus 9:16 (NIV)

WHY US?

About three months after Gore's accident, we met a family that was in the middle of their own near-drowning nightmare. We were honored to come back to the hospital to spend a few hours talking and praying with these strangers that we instantly identified with. While the events of their accident were different than Gore's, there were so many similarities. We witnessed them experiencing the same emotions we had so recently battled. The pain of not knowing how (or even if) God would heal their son took us right back to the rehabilitation floor where devastation and tragedy mixed with hope.

We experienced a strange set of emotions. We sought to be encouraging despite their own long odds of their son coming through the brain's healing process in a similar manner as Gore. Their precious twenty-two-month-old son with his big, bright smile and towheaded blond hair immediately grabbed our hearts, and we quickly bonded to them.

Today, Ryan continues to improve. He fights to get better. He is eating more on his own and starting to sit up independently; but most importantly, he is truly a happy little boy who laughs and plays with his brother and sister. Although unable to communicate as he used to, he understands all that his family says. His mom said, if he could talk, "I know he would tell us of his close relationship with the Lord."

It's unspeakably real to us what these families suffer although our story turned out differently. We struggle with what to pray or say. It's difficult when we hear a story of another child and people close to us ask, "Does it make you feel guilty that Gore is so fine?" And I think, Guilt *is not the word*. That is never the emotion we want to feel. We never want to discount in any way what God did. Honestly, I have questioned "why?" *Why* are we *not* the ones sitting in the hospital watching Gore breathing through a tube?

There are those whom we personally know, others we don't, families, and individuals out there who are in the midst of their own battle (whatever that might be) that haven't received the answer that they desire; they are unwavering in their faith. And if they never "get their miracle," their reprieve, their healing—they will still claim the name of Jesus. That's amazing and a true testament of faith.

Situations that befall us have nothing to do with whether we're good or bad or if we're "deserving." I don't believe God operates in that manner. If He did, then that would lend itself to thinking that we can somehow earn our salvation. Dave and I often say that if miracles occurred based on merit, we would not have Gore today. We just aren't "good enough" to deserve a blessing of that magnitude. Ephesians 2:4-5 NLT says,

> But God is so rich in mercy, and he loved us so
> much, that even though we were dead because
> of our sins, he gave us life when he raised Christ
> from the dead. (It is only by God's grace that
> you have been saved!)

He has a plan, and it may not be our plan. Just because He doesn't do things our way doesn't make Him any less God. If anything, it reminds us of who He is. He doesn't have to explain Himself to us.

In our times of despair, our family, our friends, and complete strangers provided us with prayers and scripture. Following were some of the verses that spoke to us:

Man's days are determined; you (God) have decreed the number of his months and have set limits he cannot exceed.

Job 14:5

Your eyes saw my unformed body. All the days ordained for me were written in your book before one of them came to be.

Psalm 139:16

Very truly I tell you, whoever hears my word *and* believes him who sent me has eternal *life and* will not be judged but has crossed over from *death to life*.

John 5:24 (NIV)

I make known the end from the beginning, from ancient times, what is still to come. I say "My purpose will stand, and I will do all that I please."

Isaiah 46:10 (NIV)

Who can speak and have it happen if the Lord has not decreed it?

Lamentations 3:37 (NIV)

GORE'S IMPACT

We've received countless letters, cards, and e-mails about how Gore's story impacted others. Each one touched us because not only did you pray so faithfully, but you also chose to share your personal experiences. We read every one of them, and each story is humbling. Below is a handful of them, mainly from people who rode this roller coaster alongside us. Each presents a different perspective of the experience. But first, let's start with some final thoughts from Dave.

Dave: During Gores's tragedy, there were several things that struck me as subtle instances of God's involvement. While the word *miracle* is tossed around loosely for many unlikely occurrences today, we believe we witnessed a perfectly orchestrated, modern-day miracle at the hand of God. These "little" illustrations constantly encouraged God's presence.

Coach David Wood was given eyes that can see fish in the water unlike any fisherman I know. While trudging through the ditch far away from where Gore fell in, and covering an area that had already been part of the frantic search, he saw a small white flash that he thought was a piece of trash but turned out to be Gore's diaper. He was pinned under a log and submerged about eighteen inches underneath the surface. God placed Coach there.

Gore's path down the ditch included passing through a concrete culvert. There were four round culverts, each approximately eighteen inches in diameter, running side by side (they were removed shortly after the accident). One of these was caved in with no water flowing through it, two were obstructed with sticks and branches and other debris, although water still flowed readily through them, and one flowed with little interference. That was the one unobstructed culvert that Gore's body could pass through. If he had gone through any of the others, he most certainly would have been stuck amidst the debris and not found until the powerful ditch was shut down.

The mosquitoes run rampant in Gunnison in July. While Mary Lynn stepped in to pray over Gore at the CPR site, she noticed Suzanne's back covered in mosquitoes. She didn't dare swat at them at risk of interfering with the CPR counting/breathing. The day following the tragedy, Mary Lynn apologized to Suzanne for the fact that she must be covered in bites. Suzanne seemed confused as she showed Mary Lynn that she didn't have a single mosquito bite.

What if Lily had her back turned when Gore reached for his tube? Based on his condition, he wasn't moving, but when he did, he was posturing. This one sporadic movement was the basis for the doctors deciding to pursue the hypothermic treatment. Thankfully, she saw it and acted on it.

In the midst of the hypothermic treatment, a few different people sent me a text indicating that when you type GORE on a telephone keypad, it also spells HOPE.

I was half-asleep when listening to Lukas and Amy talk softly on the second night (Wednesday). When discussing the importance of quality CPR, Lukas said, "I wonder if that is why your dad went to medical school." That moment helped me see the situation differently. I thought, *God, You're here, aren't You? Was that really part of Your plan from long ago? You truly can orchestrate something this big.* It was so profound to me from a twenty-six-year-old pediatric intensive care unit nurse.

We were surrounded and absolutely astonished by people's prayers. Throughout our hospital stay, we learned literally hundreds of people that we didn't even know were praying for Gore's recovery. Friends of friends, churches of distant relatives in other states, acquaintances, and people that don't normally pray at all prayed for Gore. It was humbling that so many would share in our grief.

About two weeks into the ordeal, my sister Sherri came to the hospital and witnessed Gore in rehab when he wasn't even sitting on his own. Amy's heart ached to see Gore's smile. Unbeknownst to us, Sherri had been praying specifically for Gore's smile, and later that day was the first time Gore smiled.

Why did Gore have a picture frame in his room at home since he was born that said "Miracle" on the bottom of it?

In September following Gore's accident, we were invited to the *Today Show* in New York City. NBC had arranged for a driver to pick us up at the airport. When we arrived, there was a guy holding the "Otteson" sign that would drive us to our hotel. He introduced himself as Gor. We all just stared disbelievingly, so he said it again and spelled it. Different spelling, but what are the chances of that?

David Graupman: Our kids affectionately call him Donald Duck because he often talks just like him to get a laugh out of everyone. David had been wading the ditch at the opposite end of where Coach found Gore. As Mary Lynn put our kids to bed that terrible night, David sat in our cabin quietly staring at the wall weighing everything that he ever dared to believe.

Before the incident, David described his faith in this way:

> Suzanne is very strong in her faith. Me, well I am self-described as an on-the-fence Christian. I have faith there is a God and conduct my life the best I can based on Christian principles but have always yearned for something concrete that I could hang my hat on.

Now? "As for me and my faith...well, I am off the fence."

Mary Lynn Saxon: People toss around the word *miracle* like it fits neatly in a box with a red bow on it. The problem with the little box is that it eventually gets stowed away with all the other boxes in our lives to collect dust because we have moved on. After Gore drowned, I almost got irritated at the ease with which the word rolled off people's tongues. Like, "It's just a miracle. Gore is okay." Or, "Children are such a miracle"—as if one can sum up such phenomena in this small word and move on to the next topic while I was left to relive and recount exactly what kind of miracle it was. I believed

God performed miracles before Gore's incident, but I didn't grasp the magnitude of just how powerful He is and how He longs to show up in miraculous ways when we have faith. That evening of July 6, it was as if God and His host of angels touched down on that bank and did the unimaginable. I truly believe His hand reached down from heaven and flooded that spot where Gore was lying lifeless.

> I am doing what I said I would do, what I solemnly swore I'd do that day when I was in so much trouble. All believers, come here and listen, let me tell you what God did for me. I called out to Him with my mouth. He most surely did listen, He came on the double when He heard my prayer.
>
> Psalm 66:13-20 (The Message)

On the day I left the hospital, Amy told me how strongly she believes God performs miracles and that she would pray we'd have a baby. In June, we had decided to end our battle with fertility treatment in hopes of a third child. Tommy and I had been blessed with two healthy girls through fertility and wouldn't greedily ask for more after we had a failed attempt in February. We felt He had made it clear it was time to cease and save our money. When Amy said she'd pray, I dismissed her statement with, "Well, let's just praise God for what He did for Gore and that He gave him back to us! You actually have your son!" I couldn't even go there, as I knew we would be processing this miracle for some time.

July, August, and September passed in a blur as my emotions from the summer kicked in. It wasn't until my skinny jeans no longer fit and I craved and devoured everything in sight that I knew something was peculiar. I immediately called Amy and said, "You just paid me back."

On April 27, 2011, Tag Godfrey Saxon was born. Tag stands for T, Thomas (my husband); A, Amy; and G, Gore. He's not only a reminder of my miracle but of Gore's as well. Experiencing a miracle of the magnitude of what happened with Gore, it grows your faith to ask for the unthinkable.

On the one-year anniversary of Gore's accident, it was hard to know how to feel. There were so many mixed emotions as we replayed the events from the previous year. On that day, God showed me this verse as a reminder to celebrate Him and shout it to the world!

> Bless our God, O peoples! Give Him a thunderous welcome! Didn't He set us on the road to life? Didn't He keep us out of the ditch? He trained us first, passed us like silver through refining fires, brought us into hardscrabble country, pushed us to our very limit, road tested us inside and out, took us to hell and back; Finally He brought us to this well watered place.
>
> Psalm 66:8-12 (The Message)

Corrie Casey, RN, BSN, CCRN: As a PICU nurse for almost nine years, I have witnessed countless tragedies. Out of need for self-preservation, I figure out a way to rationalize. It's easier when you can blame a child's injury on someone or something. When there's nothing to blame, or there's a well-functioning family that loves their child with complete abandon, or when cancer suddenly appears, it's easy to lose sight of a God that has His hand and purpose in everything. A couple of years ago, a wise pastor told me that in these moments God is simply asking for us to trust Him. So much of the gospel and God's plan revolves around trust, not so much specifics but trusting that He has the best plans and purposes. The Ottesons' case was hard from the beginning because there was no blame to place, only an accident. A quick blip in God's plan that in the moment felt very confusing and scary.

When I walked in and met Dave and Amy that first day, my immediate impressions were a mom that was maintaining an incredibly controlled hysteria and a grieving father who was disciplined enough to hide his true emotions from his wife. I was struck at how loving it was that his only show of grief was when he walked down the hall to the bathroom. I'd see his head sag and his shoulders get a little lower under the weight of what was going on in Room 15.

Almost every person that heard Gore's story thought the same thing, that we were prolonging the inevitable and potentially giving Dave and Amy false hope. By the end, almost everyone was readily able to admit that, cooling or no cooling, Gore's recovery was a miracle. This wasn't what was "supposed" to happen per science. The scientific facts dictated this should have led to death, yet here he was, alive. When Gore woke up, Lukas and I exchanged glances. With no words spoken, we knew that we were witnessing something unexplainable—something completely and utterly at the hand of God. In the midst of recurring tragedy in the hospital, I often think about Gore. What an amazing story to witness, affirming God's ability to work far beyond my imagination, and all He is asking is that I trust Him.

In witnessing reactions from families, the way Dave and Amy chose to respond was unique. It wasn't to become overly religious and repeatedly insist that God was going to give them a miracle. They understood so deeply that God was God. Win or lose with Gore, God was in control.

The ambulance was on scene only forty-seven seconds— "the fastest EMS turnaround in Gunnison County history," Undersheriff Randy later said proudly. Our understanding is that normally EMTs would have tried to keep him there and continue trying to resuscitate him in the field, but two factors changed the game plan. One, he's a *child*, and thus he was more portable. Two, they knew he was down for a long period of time in *cold* water. As a result, Erik Forsythe and his EMS crew chose to prepare equipment in the ambulance and attempt picking him up as fast as they could in hopes of revival at the hospital.

Erik Forsythe, NREMT-P: With every minute that goes by in situations of cardiac arrest, the chance of survival drops 7 to 10 percent. Therefore, we always remember the phrase "seconds matter." While it takes time to transport adults, we knew because of Gore's age he was "portable." The fact that I ran to pick him up was unique too because that is not "standard procedure"— we want to stay calm in these high-adrenaline scenarios. We never know what kind of situation we are walking into, but our training is to not run into a dangerous scene. Obviously in Gore's circumstance, this all changed when the ambulance could only drive so far back on the property; I had to run the rest of the way to the ditch and do what we call "load and go." I literally picked him up in my arms and, cradling him, ran back to the waiting ambulance.

In my twenty years in emergency medicine, I've never experienced a case like Gore's. When another staff member informed me that Gore woke up, I cried. The odds were *so* stacked against him. I thought of my own two children and couldn't have been more overjoyed for him and his family.

To this day, Gore has been the only child I've ever had to resuscitate. I've done CPR frequently on adults but never a small child. It was emotional, but there is no time to have those emotions in the midst of doing your job. You have to stay focused, and I credit my training for that. Later, I could decompress and process my emotions, but right then, every second counted.

Even on bad days, I remember Gore and tell myself, "Everything does work out sometimes." He is an inspiration.

———◈———

Tisha Barnes, RRT: When I saw Gore, memories of past drowning cases surfaced in my mind. I prayed he wouldn't have the same fate, where the only sign of life was merely a beating heart and basic brain function. He was cold and ghostly white. Tears came to my eyes when I heard Amy in the ER room, screaming. The sounds broke me down. Being a mother myself, I couldn't fathom such heartache; it's a mother's worst nightmare. I remember Amy's dad standing there, looking at Gore from a distance. His arms were crossed and his hand on his mouth, obviously in shock.

Everyone in the trauma room was determined, giving our all to this little boy. When Gore tried to breathe on his own, we were relieved but heartbroken in the same moment. We wanted this little boy to live a quality life but knew that the chances were slim.

When Gore visits us every July, dancing down the hallways and grinning, my reasons for working in health care are reaffirmed. His success story and the hope it brings is one of the best parts of the job. I am a stronger person because of it.

Because of the improbability of survival and outstanding quality of life, I know if God wanted Gore in heaven, he would've done it. But God raised him up. Gore has a purpose here on earth.

Randy Barnes, Undersheriff: In 1995, I responded to my first drowning call. When I arrived, EMS and off-duty fire fighters worked on her for a long time before we got her heart started. However, the next few months were difficult as the girl's quality of life completely changed.

Sometimes I cannot understand why we do what we do when we do it. God has a reason for everything. As a first responder—whether in law enforcement, EMS, or fire—you always have to keep in the back of your mind that you're here to do what you've been trained for. The hardest part is trying to understand when the best of your abilities still doesn't help.

Gore's case was tough. As with medicine, you have to distance yourself from the emotions of the job. What was harder is that I had a child that same age. On the flip side, when it comes to this call, we brag about the details: forty-seven seconds on scene, grabbing the mom and throwing her into the ambulance, telling the mom that Gore can hear her talk positively. Then there's the miracle. It will forever touch our lives. Seeing Gore every year is one of the best parts of our job. He's proof that sometimes the best of our abilities *do* yield outstanding results.

Barb Malloy, RN, CEN: That moment Gore was brought to us, lifeless and cold, almost paralyzed me.

As I told Amy, I was immediately driven by God's voice, so present and clear in my mind.

"Out of obedience to God, I laid hands on your son and prayed while they tried to resuscitate him," I had said.

Amy said she was struck and touched by that statement. She responded, "What if because you were obedient in that chaotic moment, God heard your prayers, allowing you to see His powerful healing? I believe your prayers made all the difference in the world."

Those prayers did not fall on deaf ears. I shared this verse with Amy: "If God is for us, who can be against us?" (Romans 8:31), and the fact God hears the cry of His people; he rewards those who seek Him.

I know that scripture is for the Ottesons. It's a promise I have faith in. No matter what scientific/medical theory anyone has about Gore's recovery, none of it makes any sense. Little Gore is a miracle from the living God.

———◆———

James Dreiling: Even today, as we write this book over two years later, a man named James spoke in our church. We had never met or seen him before. He spoke prior to our Communion and gave a quick overview of his upbringing and his life in the navy doing search and rescue for several years. Now married with two small children, he described how he had returned to church in 2010 after many years of not walking with God. He told of three things that took place that year that had a dramatic effect on his life, causing him to view God and his relationship with Him differently.

"I saw God at work in some very real ways," he began. Although I was listening intently to his first point, my ears perked up at his second. "The second of these three events was that a little boy named Gore, who was in my son's class here at church, had drowned. For reasons that no doctor could explain, he lived and was perfectly normal."

Gore's accident had a profound effect on him, helping lure him back to the Lord.

I started to cry as I heard this man telling his story, realizing that I had no idea who this person was in my own church, yet Gore's story helped change his life. God had used His mighty display of healing and power to draw one of his lost to Him.

Resuming Normalcy and Changing Perspective

On July 4, 2011, one year after Gore's accident, we were back in Gunnison at our annual family celebration. It was seven fifteen—the same time of night that the ambulance had arrived. Suddenly we began to hear sirens. Search and Rescue arrived and parked right in front of our property, and then came the ambulance. It was déjà vu. As the ambulance backed into our drive to turn around, the emotion of it all hit me, and I realized others as well.

As the panic set in, I looked around quickly as if to triple check that all of our kids were there, even though I could see them. The rescuers were looking for some rafters that weren't accounted for. Just as before, everyone jumped up and headed to the river to help search; the four-wheelers started to roar, and the bad nightmare flooded back. Some of us stayed behind and tried to withhold the emotions. I felt silly for my reaction until I realized I wasn't the only one that it hit like that. I saw Jody's tears and David Graupman's face as he came to hug me. They were thinking and feeling the same way. Just the sounds of the sirens, the time of night, the exact same type of evening, almost exactly one year later, and then the sight of that ambulance on our property overwhelmed us.

To this day, I immediately pull over when I see an ambulance, wondering what that person and his or her family is experiencing. To those not moving out of the way, I say into my windshield, "Pull over, people!" If Ryan is with me, she'll ask, "Mommy, are you crying again?" I hide behind my sunglasses as I shake my head.

That night, as I held Gore, I thought about God's amazing grace. As the whole nightmarish scene from a year before rolled through my head, I was reminded of what could have been but also how much I believed God was present in those moments. Our perspective is different, but it's not always perfect. I'd love to say that I wake up every day so full of joy and contentment and with a perfect "happy heart," as we say to our kids. But sadly, my human nature gets in the way, and I fall into the trap of being discontent or unhappy about this or that. It's pathetic but true. I have to stop and remind myself of how blessed we are.

Several times that same summer, we crossed the bridge over the irrigation ditch, and Gore would stop and tell us about the "water," how he went "swimming," and how it was "cold." He'd make motions like he was falling down and water was flowing over his face. It usually went something like, "Me down. Water face. Cold swim." As much as it surprised us all, none of us said much. Dave and I both don't want to plant ideas in his head but are curious about what he'll remember and tell us.

As I sat with Gore on my lap a few months later watching a "Shark Week" special on Discovery Channel, a young boy had been bitten by a shark and was carried into a helicopter. Excited, Gore started saying, "Me! Me! Me! Ride!" and pointed at the TV. He then did the same thing when they showed the boy on the operating table with a breathing tube in his mouth—"Me! Me!"

Who knows if this is from seeing pictures or actually visiting the helicopter? But then he looked at me sadly and said, "Cry." I certainly did a lot of that. But what I would give to know what happened in that water! After the accident, a friend of mine sent me a card with a picture of a child's hand resting in a larger hand. Instantly, I imagined Jesus sitting holding Gore's little hand. We believe He comforted Gore during those hours and days that he appeared to have no life in him. I sometimes look at Gore and wonder if he has been where we long to be.

EPILOGUE

Every one of us has encountered some form of tragedy. We have all endured pain. Maybe it's a broken heart, a long battle with a relentless disease, an addiction, or the loss of a child or spouse. We know what it is to walk through deep valleys. If you haven't, you walk a fortunate road that not many get to travel.

Certainly in Gore's story, we had the best medical staff, knowledge, and equipment available to us, and we never want to discredit that. It took *every* person, their abilities, and their refusal to give up for this outcome. But still, God gets the glory. We are so thankful every day for the gift we were given, yet we realize that other families have experienced tragedies and were not so fortunate in the outcome. It's heartbreaking to know these stories and try to make sense of why they don't end up the way that we desire. We certainly don't deserve the gift that we were given, and we don't believe that we will understand why God was so merciful to us on this side of heaven.

This is the story of our tragedy that, by God's grace, was turned into a miracle. Our purpose is that Gore's story is encouraging, that it gives hope, and that, ultimately, people can see the power of God's healing hand and the power of prayer. We can't experience what we have and move on or forget. It's a story that goes from tragedy to triumph about a precocious little towheaded boy that is living life to the fullest without any fear.

> Now God has us where he wants us, with all the time in this world and the next to shower grace and kindness upon us in Christ Jesus. Saving is all his idea, and all his work. All we do is trust him enough to let him do it. It's God's gift from start to finish! We don't play the major role. If we did, we'd probably go around bragging that we'd done the whole thing! No, we neither make nor save ourselves. God does both the making and saving.
>
> Ephesians 2:7-9 (The Message)

THANK YOU

Gunnison Valley Hospital and First Responders: Thank you will never be enough. Our appreciation for all that you did in that critical first hour cannot be verbalized. Thank you for never giving up. Your efficiency, expertise, and emotional support can't be measured. Dr. Sherman, Barb, Tisha, Chris, Erik, Matt, John, Brian, Sara, Jason, Ellen, Ariel, Randy, and Jim—we personally thank each one of you.

Children's Hospital Colorado: We were amazed at both the level of care and the kindness of everyone at this hospital. A special thank you to everyone in the PICU and on the rehabilitation floor. What an outstanding group of people. Thank you for doing everything possible for Gore and our family.

CareFlight 11: Thank you for taking such good care of Gore when we couldn't be with him. Your continued support of him and our family means a lot to us. Gore proudly has his Honorary Flight Crew badge up in his room.

Children's Miracle Network Hospitals at Children's Hospital Colorado Foundation: Thank you for all that you do to raise money for these kids and Children's hospitals.

Children's Medical Center: What a wonderful group of people. Thank you for caring for all three of our children and for your prayers during Gore's accident. Dr. Zavadil, we are so blessed to have you as our kids' pediatrician.

To Our Families: How do we begin to thank you? It's not enough. We are thankful beyond words for each one of you. You were there—day and night, physically and in prayer. We are blessed by your love and support.

Bear Valley Church: Thank you to the Bear Valley Church body that was so strong in enveloping us with prayer. We were overwhelmed at the outpouring of community and the faithfulness of friends. Thank you to all of you that came to be with us in our darkest days.

CaringBridge: This is a tremendous vehicle for people to communicate in a private, specific setting. Reading the Guestbook posts on this site brightened our spirits knowing you were walking alongside us.

Corrie and Lukas: With whom we have traveled through Gore's story so many times. Thank you for your patience with us and helping us to understand the details. More importantly, for your friendship, which is invaluable.

Helen Wood: Thank you for reading and reading again and again. Your perspective and input was wonderful.

Katherine Haynes: Thank you for your friendship and getting on a plane without ever asking the question.

Mary Waugh: Thank you for coming across the country with perfect timing to be with an old friend in our time of need.

Mary Lynn Saxon: How do I thank you for being there that night and in all the days that followed? You were with Gore when he needed it most. Thank you for believing in this book and not letting it go— making sure God gets all the glory.

Rikki Frazier: Thank you for coming to the hospital day after day to pray and support us and for continuing to share Gore's story.

Our friends: You thought of everything—prayers, cards, visits, gifts, meals… You mowed our lawn, you cleaned our house, and you left no stone unturned. Thank you for your true friendship, for constantly lifting us up.

Ashley Roy: We could not have done this without you as the Creative Project Director. Your commitment, diligence, organization, and professional knowledge were invaluable. Thank you for making this book a reality.

To those fighting the good fight: You not only inspire us, but you remind us to be thankful and humble for our blessings. Mandy, Kelly, the Hoffmans, Jim, and to so many more—to all of you who haven't "gotten your miracle" but keep fighting while always claiming the name of Jesus. You're amazing!

ENDNOTE

Beth Moore, *Believing God*, (Nashville: LifeWay Press, 2002), 9-11.